Be Transformed Revised

Discovering God's Solutions to Life's Problems

2020 revision

Scope Ministries International

Copyright 2020 Scope Ministries International, Inc.
All Rights Reserved
All rights reserved. N part of this publication may be reproduced, stored in a retrieval system, or transmitted in any form by any means - electronic, digital, mechanical, photocopy, recording, or any other - except for prior, written permission of the Publisher's Media Department.

ISBN 978-109043479-1

Copyright 1998, 2001, 2005, 2007, 2019, 2020 Scope Ministries International, INC.

Preface

This workbook was originally written to be a personal aid to those seeking spiritual help for life's problems through attending a Scope Discovery Group. A discovery group is a small group that investigates God's Word and how it applies to emotional, spiritual, and relational needs. There are two segments to the discovery group: the lesson presentation and small group interaction. Its purpose is to help people overcome life's challenges.

These lessons will introduce you to a new way of thinking about your problems, whether they be personal, emotional, or relational. For each lesson there are five daily assignments that are intended to help you interact with God in such a way that you receive understanding of underlying causes and direction in dealing with them.

Be Transformed lays a Biblical foundation of truth that opens the door to an experiential relationship with God. Whether you choose to use this individually or in a small group, it is our prayer that the Holy Spirit will be your counselor and will use this material to draw you into a more intimate relationship with your Heavenly Father, resulting in a transformed life.

The Be Transformed lessons are available on video, along with Be Transformed leaders' guides. To find out how to start a Be Transformed discovery group or to order materials, contact:

Scope Ministries International
700 NE 63rd Street
Oklahoma City, OK 73105-6410
USA
405.843.7778
Website: www.scopeministries.org

This workbook attempts to lay a proper Biblical foundation for a healthy relationship with God and to demonstrate how God's Word applies to the entire scope of life but it does not attempt to address all different types of problems we encounter.

Acknowledgments

This workbook was originally was written to enable our ministry to meet the needs of an increasing number of people seeking help in relating to God in the midst of their problems. As God healed broken lives and marriages, more and more people requested copies of the workbook. To our great delight, many have used this material in their personal lives, their churches, and their ministries.

Over the course of the development of this workbook, many have contributed to this final form. Scope staff have persevered through changes and rewrites with great patience. Their critiques and suggestions have been invaluable to the fine-tuning of this work.

We deeply appreciate those who have shared their stories with us of how God has changed their lives as they have worked through the daily assignments. Thank you for being transparent and letting us see the marvelous work God is doing in your hearts. May there be many, many more like you in the future.

Many others, too numerous to mention, have helped make this book a reality. Many have prayed, given financially and encouraged this into existence. This project is a beautiful picture of team effort and the necessity of diversity in the Body of Christ. May it build up Christ's Bride and prepare her for His return.

Recently it became evident that a few errors (mostly work useage, spelling, etc.) needed to be clarified and addressed. It is our hope that this revised version will clarify His life changing Life and truth.

Scope Ministries International

Be Transformed
Revised Version

Preface

Acknowledgments

Table of Contents

Introduction

Part One: The Truth - God's Perspective

Lesson 1	The Truth About Lies	page 7
Lesson 2	The Truth About the Cross	page 31
Lesson 3	The Truth About Your New Identity	page 63
Lesson 4	The Truth About God	page 87
Lesson 5	The Truth About the Holy Spirit	page 113

Part Two: Freedom in Life

Lesson 6	Freedom with Emotions	page 137
Lesson 7	Freedom in Forgiveness	page 161
Lesson 8	Freedom from Performance Based Acceptance	page 187

Part Three: Living in Truth and Freedom

Lesson 9	A Life Transformed	page 211

Copyright 1998, 2001, 2005, 2007, 2019, 2020 Scope Ministries International, INC.

Introduction

Dear Reader,

You are about to embark upon a thrilling adventure of Christian living. Since 1973, Scope Ministries International (Scope) has been taking life-changing truths from the Bible and developing them into practical solutions that transform lives

From its inception, Scope has sought to deal with solutions rather than symptoms, and with people's potential rather than their problems. The workbook, Be Transformed, is the result of many years of observation and research. Designed not simply to impart information but to bring transformation, it has been instrumental in seeing thousands of lives changed.

Be Transformed brings several crucial distinctives into play. First, it is centered around Christ and His sufficiency. Second, it is based upon the authority and sufficiency of Scripture. Third, it guides individuals into a practical, life-changing experience through the renewing of their belief systems.

The dynamic behind the success of this workbook is its foundation of the Living Word and the Word of God. Biblical truth has been turned into therapeutic tools, which, in turn, have been developed into transferable concepts. This allows the power of God to be the vital force in the life-changing process presented in Be Transformed.

The Bible teaches that God did not send His Son to die simply to get man to Heaven, but rather to get God out of Heaven into man! In other words Be Transformed stands upon God's ability to reproduce Himself within us.

Be Transformed is based on three basic great doctrines of the Bible.

> Be Transformed is based on the fact of the Deity of Jesus Christ.
>
> Be Transformed is based on the authority of the Word of God.
>
> Be Transformed is based upon the sufficiency of Christ and Scripture.

During the next few weeks, as you learn and absorb the truths presented, you will discover personally the transforming power of Christ the living Word. Remember, God never fails—you will be transformed!

March 2020

The Truth About Lies

And do not be conformed to this world, but be transformed by the renewing of your mind, that you may prove what the will of God is, that which is good and acceptable and perfect.

Romans 12:2 NASB

Lesson One

A Transformed Life

Towards the end of my college years, I realized that I had two possible directions: run to God or run away from God. It all depended upon what I believed about everything.

My parents separated when I was 6 years old, and I was raised in a non-Christian home by my mother. I felt like I was a burden to her because she had to begin working to support us when she and my dad divorced. I saw my dad inconsistently, and I always felt as if he visited me from obligation, not because he truly wanted to see me.

I always felt that something was wrong with me, and I struggled for acceptance as long as I can remember, trying everything, both good and bad, to get it. I tried to act like an adult rather than a child so I wouldn't bother my mom. I tried to be a perfect and proper person — a polite daughter, a good student, and a skilled athlete. I excelled at school, and I tried not to cause trouble, but I also drank, smoked and partied with the wild kids. I looked everywhere to everyone for the acceptance I craved.

As a college student, I even became very religious, and I worked at religion the same way I worked at being a daughter - doing the right thing so that God would be pleased with me. I was still dissatisfied and empty. My beliefs about God were directly related to my life experiences, so I was unable to have a relationship with Him. I believed that I was just as much an inconvenience to God as I had been to my mother. I believed that God was just like my dad — not involved in my life except for the occasional appearance motivated by obligation rather than by love. I also felt that God had failed me. I had done all the right things, but I wasn't rewarded. When I really needed His help, I felt as if He had abandoned me. I began to question His goodness.

I felt like a failure, and I became depressed to the point of suicide.

to be continued...

The Truth about Lies - Lesson One

We all face problems every day, and we all struggle from time to time in our Christian lives. Jesus assured us that we would have trouble in this world, but He also promised that He would be with us and would make us overcomers (John 16:33). Only Jesus has the power and authority to overcome the problems of this world, and only Jesus can overcome the personal, internal problems we struggle with each day. Our Creator understands us better than we understand ourselves. He came that we might have and enjoy life.

> *I came that they might have and enjoy life, and have it in abundance (to the full, till it overflows).* John 10:10b AMP

Why then, are we experiencing so little victory and joy in our lives? Why are so many Christians plagued with personal problems? Why are we not experiencing the abundant life that Jesus promised? Whether we are struggling with emotional, relational, behavioral, or spiritual problems, Jesus is the answer and has revealed the solution in His Word. The Bible gives us everything we need to live by pointing us to the Source of abundant life. Through the lessons and daily assignments, you will discover just how relevant God's Word is to the needs and problems you face every day. The assignments are designed to help you interact with God and receive from Him the wisdom and strength to overcome life's challenges.

God's Word Reveals the Truth About Lies

The solution to the problems we struggle with can be discovered by addressing the root of our problems as revealed in God's Word. Romans 1:25 identifies man's basic root problem.

> *For they exchanged the truth of God for a lie, and worshipped and served the creature rather than the Creator.* Romans 1:25 NASB

The lie began in the Garden when Eve believed God was withholding good and wisdom. She believed she could determine good and evil apart from Him. Adam chose to join Eve rather than believe God. They both decided to determine for themselves what is true and what is good. (see Genesis 3:1-7). The consequences of their choice were passed on to us all. We have all tried to live life independent of God by relying on our own reason.

The root problems we need to address are the lies we have believed about God, ourselves, life, and others. The written word of God, the Bible, is an extension of the Living Word, Jesus Christ. It shows us how God created us to live in relationship with Him. It exposes the lies we

Copyright 1998, 2001, 2005, 2007, 2019, 2020 Scope Ministries International, INC.

Regardless of our circumstances Jesus is the Solution.

"Grace and truth continually come through Him."

John 1:17b

> *Though we have problems, we are not our problems. They affect us but exist apart from us. They are not our identity.*
>
> *"The Spirit who lives in us is greater than the spirit who lives in the world."*
>
> *1 John 4:4*

have believed and reveals the truth. Scripture addresses more than behavior, it gives us God's viewpoint of life.

Therefore, we can:

- Learn to address life's problems and issues from God's perspective

The whole Bible was given to us by inspiration from God and is useful to teach us what is true and to make us realize what is wrong in our lives; it straightens us out and helps us do what is right. 2 Timothy 3:16 LB

- Recognize that the Bible addresses not only our behaviors, but also our thoughts and beliefs

- Develop correct beliefs about God, self, life, and others

- Learn to think as God thinks

If you abide in My word, then you are truly disciples of Mine; and you shall know the truth, and the truth shall make you free.
John 8:31b-32 NASB

If Truth is what sets us free, then it must be lies that produce bondage in our lives. Jesus desires to speak truth to our hearts and set us free from whatever bondage we are in. The purpose of these lessons is to help recognize the lies that are hindering you from experiencing the abundant life that is yours in Christ.

Our Beliefs Influence and Control Our Lives

God created us as believing beings and addresses us as such. Scripture speaks to us concerning our beliefs about God, ourselves, life, and others. A belief is an assumption we hold to be true: a presupposition or conviction. We do not usually question our beliefs and are often not even consciously aware of them. We have beliefs about everything. We do not live by animal instincts, but by beliefs that have been developed and reinforced throughout our lives. Our beliefs cause us to process certain information and block other information.

Copyright 1998, 2001, 2005, 2007, 2019, 2020 Scope Ministries International, INC.

The Truth about Lies

A Belief That...	May Result In...
Money provides security and happiness	workaholisim, materialism, greed, dishonesty, stealing
To be happy I must be married	unhappiness being single, unrealistic expectations of spouse, discontentment with spouse
I am the way I am; I can't change	feelings of shame, guilt, hopelessness, inferiority, passivity, loss of creativity, victimization, self-centeredness, pride, manipulation
Failure deserves to be punished	criticalness, judgementalism, self-destructive behavior, fear of failure, procrastination, unwillingness to take risks, fear of punishment
The more I do for God, the more He will love and bless me	legalistic religious activity, serving God to earn His acceptance, spiritual burnout; feeling unacceptable to God, self-righteousness, spiritual pride
My worth is determined by what I do and what others think of me	An excessive drive to succeed, competitive, high achiever, comparing self with others, pride: superiority, inferiority

A lie believed as truth will affect your life as if it were true— even though it is a lie.

What we believe directly affects the quality of our lives.

As we grow up, we develop beliefs about everything. Our experiences with our parents, environment, family, school, and peers have all influenced what we believe. We have developed basic life beliefs about:

- Who we are
- Whom we can trust
- What is good or bad
- What we are worth
- What our purpose in life is
- What God is like.

Copyright 1998, 2001, 2005, 2007, 2019, 2020 Scope Ministries International, INC.

The Truth about Lies

> *A faulty belief system is like a lens which distorts our perception of reality.*

A group of beliefs form a belief system through which we see the world. It is similar to wearing sunglasses which colors the landscape. We accept or reject new information based on our basic life beliefs. Our belief system determines how we perceive life.

If a person grows up being told they are worthless, they will be more likely to believe they are inferior to others. This belief can limit the talents and abilities God has given them. The result can be shown in having difficulty accepting a compliment.

Our beliefs control how we respond to life.

We live out what we believe to be true about ourselves. What we believe affects our actions, motives, thoughts, words, emotions and relationships. We make choices based upon our beliefs. As others respond to our behavior, their reactions tend to reinforce our belief system. Our perception of reality is based on the beliefs we hold.

Our Belief System Is Faulty

Most of our beliefs were formed before we had any awareness of God.

At birth we had no conscious understanding of God so we formed our own belief system without regard to His Truth. We grew up living independently of God while relying on our own understanding—which has created and developed our faulty belief system. Our faulty beliefs often seem more true and rational than God's Word.

> *There is a way which seems right to man, but its end is the way of death.* Proverbs 14:12 NASB

> *They exchanged the glory of the incorruptible God for an image in the form of corruptible man . . .* Romans 1:23

Our belief system is affected by the world's influence and Satan. Satan uses the influences of this world to harm us and to mold our thinking. Satan's greatest strategy is to deceive us to keep us in bondage to sin destroying our lives. Satan tempts us to act on wrong emotions, thoughts and beliefs thus reinforcing the wrong beliefs we already have.

> *For the god of this world has blinded the unbelievers' minds [that they should not discern the truth], preventing them from seeing the illuminating light of the Gospel [good news] of the glory of Christ (the Messiah), Who is the Image and Likeness of God.* 2 Corinthians 4:4 Amplified

> *The thief [Satan] comes only to steal, kill, and destroy . . .* John 10:10a NASB

page 12

Copyright 1998, 2001, 2005, 2007, 2019, 2020 Scope Ministries International, INC.

> *He [the devil] was a murderer from the beginning, and does not stand in the truth, because there is no truth in him. Whenever he speaks a lie, he speaks from his own nature; for he is a liar, and the father of lies.*
> John 8:44b NASB

As new creations in Christ we don't have to continue believing these lies. Why?

Our belief system can be changed.

We can learn to recognize and replace our faulty beliefs with God's Truth.

God has provided a way to free us from our old belief system. He has given us His Word, so we can recognize and change our beliefs and experience healing. Our lives change as we allow God to reveal and renew our minds (beliefs).

The more we believe what God says, the more we recognize and reject false beliefs or lies. This allows us to experience joy and peace. Believing and acting on the truth sets us free to live righteously and to love and experience God.

> *Don't copy the behavior and customs of this world, but let God transform you into a new person by changing the way you think. Then you will learn to know God's will for you, which is good and pleasing and perfect.* Romans 12:2a NLT

God does not tell us to renew our behavior or our emotions. He tells us to renew our minds because the problem lies with our belief system. What we truly believe is revealed by how we respond to life's circumstances.

What we know about God can be very different from what we believe about Him. When God reveals a lie we can then choose to reject it and replace it with His truth. There is no shame or condemnation in recognizing we have believed a lie. God delights when His children gain a more accurate understanding of His character.

The process of renewing our minds is not a matter of deep introspection nor is it a matter of replacing our negative thoughts with positive ones. This renewing process involves our relating to God and depending on Him to reveal lies and teach us what is true. This renewal is only possible through the work of the Holy Spirit. We will talk about the Holy Spirit in more detail in future lessons.

> *But the Helper, the Holy Spirit, whom the Father will send in My name, He will teach you all things . . .* John 14:26a NASB

The Truth about Lies

*But when He, the Spirit of truth comes, He will guide you into all the truth...*John 16:13a NASB

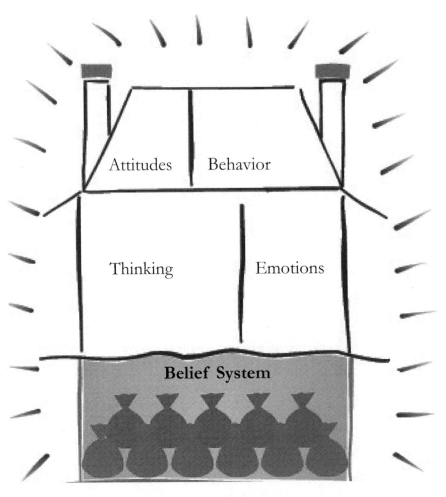

What we believe is revealed by how we live, not by what we know.

A couple built a new house in a neighborhood where no garbage service was available. They stored their garbage in their basement so it would be out of sight and out of their way until they could haul it to the dump. While they spent their time and energy furnishing their new home and landscaping their yard, the trash began to pile up. The day finally arrived when they invited all their friends and family over to see their new home. Even though the couple's home was exceptionally clean and was filled with beautiful furnishings, their guests were not impressed. The odor from the basement had permeated every room. Cleaning would do little good until they got rid of the garbage in the basement. This illustrates how our corrupted belief system affects all areas of our life. It first affects our thinking and emotions, then our attitudes and behavior. Until we consciously recognize and reject the lies we have believed, the truth will have little impact on our lives.

We Can Experience Joy and Peace

The Truth about Lies

Allowing Jesus to change our thoughts and beliefs will bring healing to our emotions, freedom from destructive behavior, and love for God and others.

Our wrong beliefs produce negative thinking, which gives rise to painful emotions and destructive behavior. When a belief is corrected about God, self, life, others and/or Scripture, our thinking can line up with our new beliefs. This empowers us to make Godly choices, as Christ lives through us producing a transformed life.

Changing our thoughts and beliefs will eventually result in greater joy.

The more we believe what God says, the more we can experience a life of joy and peace. Problems are inevitable. We have all been hurt and wounded by others and life's circumstances. Even if these people and circumstances never change, we can still learn to have joy and peace in the midst of all situations. Allowing the truth of God's Word to change our belief system does not alter our past but can change our perspective of the past. This will transform our lives and give us hope and wisdom for the future. Here's a thought: When we receive Christ we receive His life and His past!!

> *Behold, you desire truth in the innermost being, and in the hidden part You will make me know wisdom.* Psalm 51:6 NASB

Remember, God is always present, full of compassion and grace, and willing to heal our broken hearts and lives. He desires more than we do to fill our lives with His hope, joy, and peace.

> *May the God of hope fill you with all joy and peace in your faith [beliefs], that by the power of the Holy Spirit, your whole life and outlook may be radiant with hope.*
> Romans 15:13 Phillips

The daily assignments that follow are designed to lead you to discover some of the false beliefs that are robbing you of the quality of life that keep you from enjoying your new freedom in Christ. As you do each assignment, invite Holy Spirit, to be your teacher and counselor. There is no need to be deeply introspective. God desires to reveal to you the lies that need to be rejected and the truth that needs to be received and believed. Remember, His ability to reveal His Truth is greater than our ability to discover His Truth!

> *Trust in the Lord with all your heart, and do not lean on your own understanding. In all your ways acknowledge Him, and He will make your paths straight.* Proverbs 3:5-6, NASB

Copyright 1998, 2001, 2005, 2007, 2019, 2020 Scope Ministries International, INC.

The Truth about Lies

For as a man thinks within himself, so he is. Proverbs 23:7a

Summary:

1. We are believing beings, and all of our beliefs combine to form a belief system.

2. Most of our problems stem from a faulty belief system.

3. Our beliefs affect our thinking, emotions, attitudes, and behavior.

4. We can be transformed and experience joy through the renewing of our minds by the Holy Spirit.

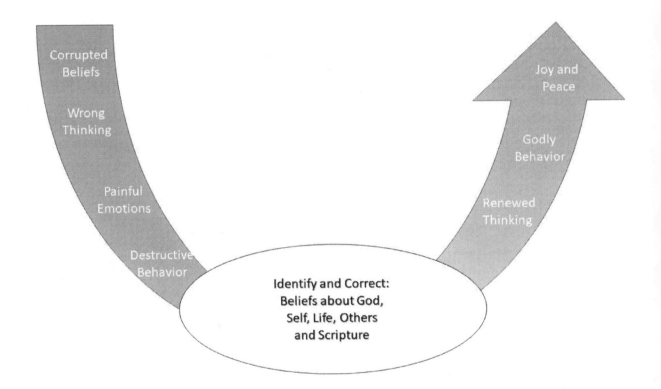

A Life Transformed, continued

When I was at my lowest point, God showed me the key to changing my life was not trying to change the outside but changing what I believed. God helped me to identify the lies that I had believed and to replace them with the truth. I began to believe that God accepts me and that I am pleasing to Him because He is in me. I began to enjoy just being with Him and talking with Him. I now enjoy life because I know He is always with me. I truly feel free to be me. As I changed my beliefs, my behavior changed. My beliefs; feelings, and passions are from God, so I don't have to worry about pleasing others and they don't have to please me. I can give freedom to those around me because they are pleasing to God and He wants me to love them as He loves me.

Choosing to reject the lie and to believe the truth that God loves and accepts me changed my life because I can and I want to have a relationship with God like that.

Now my direction in life is running to God instead of away from Him.

Katrina – Teacher

The Truth about Lies - Day One

Goal: To identify the problem from your perspective and to ask God to reveal His perspective of the problem.

All of us experience problems. Life is full of problems. Success is not the absence of problems but knowing how to respond and resolve the problems. God has not left us alone to try to overcome our problems in our own strength and wisdom. He has given us the Holy Spirit and His Word to empower and teach us.

> *Every Scripture is God-breathed (given by His inspiration) and profitable for instruction, for reproof and conviction of sin, for correction of error and discipline in obedience, [and] for training in righteousness (in holy living, in conformity to God's will in thought, purpose, and action), so that the man of God may be complete and proficient, well-fitted and thoroughly equipped for every good work.* II Timothy 3:16-17 *Amplified*

These verses tell us God's Word is sufficient and profitable to make us adequate and equipped. In other words, God's Word shows us the way or path to abundant living (teaching). God's Word shows us when we get off the path (reproof). God's Word shows us how to get back on the path (correction) and how to stay on the path (training in righteousness). This path is not merely a set of correct behaviors we are to perform. God is committed to showing us when we leave the path of correct beliefs and thoughts as well as correcting our behavior.

1. What problem do you want God to change or address in your life? (conflict in relationship, emotional struggle, habit, or behavior) Choose one.

2. How is this problem affecting you emotionally?

3. What behaviors or habits in your life are contributing to this problem?

4. How is your behavior affecting your relationships with others?

5. What are some prevailing thoughts that run through your mind when you think about your specific problem?

6. How do you see your problem affecting your relationship with God?

In time, as you seek God's perspective, you will be able to recognize the beliefs that are contributing to these problems and replace those beliefs with the truth as revealed in God's Word.

7. Write your prayer, asking God to begin showing you His perspective of your problem and any beliefs that are contributing to it.

The Truth about Lies - Day Two

Goal: To see from Scripture the effect our beliefs have on our lives.

Because we are believing beings, we each create a belief system that controls our lives. Our beliefs were formed before we had any awareness of God.

Read the account of the fall in Genesis 2:8-9, 16-17; 3:1-7.

1. What did God tell Adam in Genesis 2:16-17?

2. What did Satan imply by his question in Genesis 3:1?

3. What subtle lie did Satan use to tempt Eve to doubt what is true? (see Genesis 3:4)

4. Whom did Eve believe?

5. How did her belief affect her behavior? What were the consequences?

6. What do you think is Satan's role in forming people's beliefs today?

7. How has the fall of man affected you personally?

8. The purpose of this short Bible study is to reveal how our beliefs affect our emotions and behavior. Read each passage and write out the resulting emotion and behavior:

Person(s)	Belief	Emotion	Behavior
The Ten Spies Numbers 13:1-2,17, 20, 23-33	believed they were small and weak	Fear and inadequacy	gave bad report; unwilling to enter the Promised Land; wanted to stone Joshua, Caleb
Joshua and Caleb Numbers 13:1-2,17, 20, 23-33	believed God had given them the land and would give them the ability to take possession		
Moses Exodus 4:10-15	believed he was inadequate		
Disciples Mark 4:35-41	believed they were perishing		
Jesus Mark 4:35-41	believed His heavenly Father was in control		

9. What conclusions can you draw from these examples?

On what was each behavior based?

10. How do your beliefs compare with those in the examples above?

11. Write out a prayer asking God to reveal to you the truth from His Word.

page 22   Copyright 1998, 2001, 2005, 2007, 2019, 2020 Scope Ministries International, INC.

The Truth about Lies - Day Three

Goal: To begin uncovering some of your basic life beliefs.

1. Complete the following sentences with the first answer that comes to your mind:

I would be more successful if...

I would be satisfied if...

I would be happier if...

I would be content if...

I could never be happy if...

I would feel more secure if...

I would be more peaceful if...

2. What beliefs are revealed by your answers?

3. Choose one of your beliefs revealed in question 2 and write out your corresponding thoughts, emotions, and behaviors. See the examples below:

EXAMPLE #1: Belief: Making a lot of money means I am successful.

    Thoughts: Consumed with getting ahead, bigger house, better car, etc.

    Emotions: Feel anxious about job; angry at co-workers who seem to block goals; envious of co-workers' success; guilt

    Behavior: Workaholic, drink to relieve stress from job, not spending time with family, critical of others

EXAMPLE #2: Belief: If my spouse would change, I'd be happy.

    Thoughts: "If only he/she would . . ."
                         "Why can't he/she be more like _____'s spouse?"

                         "I'm stuck for life. This marriage is hopeless."
                         "I could never be happy married to this person."

    Emotions: Anger, hurt, rejection, resentment, revenge

    Behavior: Manipulating, nagging, withdrawing, withholding affection, demanding

Belief:

    Thoughts:

    Emotions:

    Behavior:

The Truth about Lies - Day Four

Goal: To see from God's Word how corrupted our minds were when our beliefs were formed.

1. According to the following verse, how does Paul describe the thinking of an unbeliever?

> *You walk no longer just as the Gentiles [unbelievers] also walk, in the futility of their mind [foolish and vain thinking], being darkened in their understanding [distorted reasoning], excluded [alienated] from the life of God, because of the ignorance that is in them... Ephesians 4:17b-18a NASB*

2. What knowledge did man feel it was unnecessary to retain?

> *And so, since they did not see fit to acknowledge God or approve of Him or consider Him worth the knowing, God gave them over to a base [depraved] and condemned mind to do things not proper or decent but loathsome, until they were filled (permeated and saturated) with every kind of unrighteousness . . . Romans 1:28-29a Amplified*

3. What kind of thinking did God allow to control man?

4. What knowledge do unbelievers now have?

> *For the god of this world has blinded the unbelievers' minds [that they should not discern the truth], preventing them from seeing the illuminating light of the Gospel of the glory of Christ (the Messiah), Who is the Image and Likeness of God. 2 Corinthians 4:4 Amplified*

5. On what do their minds focus?

> . . . *whose end is destruction (eternal misery), whose god is their appetite, and whose glory is in their shame, who set their minds on earthly things.   Philippians 3:19b NAS*

6. What can you conclude about the thoughts of the unsaved mind?

Note: This does not mean that every thought of man is totally disgusting, vulgar, and repulsive; however, the end result of wrong thoughts is corruption and the exclusion of God.

7. Take a moment to reflect on the following verse and to ask God to show you any anxious or hurtful thoughts that need to be rejected and replaced with God's truth. Write down any thoughts He shows you.

> *Search me, O God, and know my heart; try me and know my anxious thoughts; and see if there be any hurtful way in me, and lead me in the everlasting way. Psalm 139:23-24 NASB*

8. Write Romans 12:2 on a 3x5 card or a post-it note and place it in a prominent place where you will see it often. Each time you see this verse, personalize it as a prayer.

Sample prayer: Father, I no longer want to be conformed to the thinking of this world. I desire to be transformed by the renewing of my mind. Make me more aware of what I am thinking and show me the lies that I have been believing. I want to live out Your will, which is good, acceptable, and perfect.

The Truth about Lies - Day Five

Goal: To continue to identify some of your unique personal beliefs.

Our beliefs are shaped by our perceptions which are based on our experiences with our parents, family, school, peers, etc.

Scripture clearly states that all are born captive to sin and ignorant of Truth.

> *There is none righteous, not even one; There is none who understands, There is none who seeks for God. Romans 3:10b-11 NASB*

> *For all have sinned and fall short of the glory of God. Romans 3:23 NASB*

Growing up in a fallen world, we learn about life from our environment, experiences, and what others teach us. We learn:

- Who we are;
- Whom we can trust;
- What is good or bad;
- What we are worth;
- What our purpose is in life; and
- What God is like.

What we learn becomes our belief system by which we evaluate all new information. We accept or reject new information based on our basic life beliefs. These beliefs are like a lens through which we see life and which control our behavior.

Because our perceptions are distorted and the way we process information is distorted, many of our patterns of behaving and relating to others are also distorted. As others respond to our behavior, their reactions tend to reinforce what we believe to be true.

1. Name one significant negative life experience that has shaped what you believe about yourself.

2. List the beliefs formed from that life experience:

   Who am I?

   Whom can I trust?

   What is good or bad?

   What am I worth?

   What is my purpose in life?

3. How have these beliefs been reinforced over the years?

   Example: Growing up I was poor at math and my dad called me stupid. Kids at school would make fun of me. I hated math all through school and flunked Algebra. I chose not to go to college. I feel like such a failure but I'm afraid to try anything else. Everyone else in my family has a college degree. My dad has never indicated that he is proud of me. Now I find myself being hard on my children when they don't make A's.

4. How are these beliefs still manifested in your thoughts, emotions, behaviors, and relationships? (In other words, how do these beliefs control you? In what areas do you feel held back because of these beliefs?)

   And I (Jesus) will ask the Father, and He will give you another Helper, that He may be with you forever; that is the Spirit of truth whom the world cannot receive, because it does not behold Him or know Him, but you know Him because He abides with you, and will be in you . . . But when He, the Spirit of truth, comes, He will guide you into all the truth. John 14:16-17 NASB

5. Write out a prayer, asking the Holy Spirit to reveal the truth to you concerning these beliefs.

The Truth about Lies - Lesson One Summary

Name _____ Date _____

Answer the following questions. Turn in a copy of your answers to the small group leader.

1. Briefly describe from DAY ONE the problem with which you are presently struggling.

2. What are some of your "beliefs" that relate to your area of struggle?

3. How are these beliefs affecting you (emotionally, relationally, behaviorally)?

4. What is God showing you from this week's lesson?

5. How often do you turn to God's Word for answers to your problems?

___never___seldom___often____ very often_____ always

6. What questions do you have concerning this week's assignment?

7. Mark the graph to indicate how much of this week's assignment you completed.

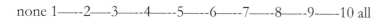
none 1—--2—--3—--4—--5—--6—--7—--8—--9—--10 all

The Truth About The Cross

You were dead in sins, and your sinful desires were not yet cut away. Then He gave you a share in the very life of Christ, for He forgave all your sins, and blotted out the charges proved against you, the list of His commandments which you had not obeyed. He took this list of sins and destroyed it by nailing it to Christ's cross.
Colossians 2:13-14 TLB

Lesson Two

A Life Transformed

My life was in constant turmoil. I was overwhelmed with fear and depression and plagued by thoughts of suicide. I was scared to do anything because it would inevitably be the wrong choice. I used drugs and alcohol to escape my pain but they just made my misery worse. I tried to fill the hole in my life with sexual relationships that just became an additional problem.

I looked everywhere for help — the occult, eastern philosophies and practices — but I just became more confused. I tried doctors, counselors, healers, psychics, Alcoholics Anonymous, and Narcotics Anonymous. Each attempt brought temporary relief, but then I would feel even worse because of a worse emotional bombardment and the terrible sense of impending doom.

I was so desperate to be free of my misery that I was pointing a gun to my head, ready to commit suicide, but I asked God for help instead. When a friend got me into a treatment program the very next day, I knew God had answered my prayer.

Even after I had been clean and sober for several years, I was still more miserable and depressed than ever. The problem wasn't the drugs and alcohol. The problem wasn't the world around me. The problem wasn't the relationships. The problem was the conflict in me.

I had to lose a lot before I was finally desperate enough to accept God's solution to my problem. I've always been aware of God's influence in my life. I knew that He was guiding me when my conscience told me that I was making bad choices, especially when I experienced the consequences. Even as a child, I knew that I wasn't here just to wander around aimlessly. I've always had an inner sense that God had a purpose for me, but I avoided it because I've always avoided responsibility.

I always knew that I eventually would turn to God, and, throughout my life, people have pointed me to a relationship with Christ. This time, when a friend started telling me about the changes Christ had made in her life, I finally listened. As she talked, I felt as if I was finally finding true hope, but I was also scared. I was scared of having to admit my faults, and I was afraid of the consequences when I actually faced what I had done and who I had become. I was afraid of change. I knew that I had to turn to God for help, but I was wavering between fear and hope.

My past had almost destroyed me, but now my future scared me. I was afraid of the new responsibilities, and I wasn't sure I could live the Christian life. Because of my old beliefs, I was still feeling the inner turmoil I had experienced all my life. I still believed that God could not accept me or love me because I was unacceptable, unlovable, and unworthy.

to be continued...

The Truth About the Cross — Lesson Two

In our previous lesson, we discovered we are believing beings. The first belief we examined was our belief about who God is, The Truth About God. Then we looked at how we are three part beings, made in His image and why that matters, The Truth About Your New Identity. In this lesson, we will discover why the Gospel is the Good News. This Good News is more than forgiveness; it is an exchange of our old, faulty life for the new, righteous life of Christ. However, many Christians are unaware of the full measure of this exchange and continue to feel miserable and defeated. These emotions occur when faulty beliefs continue to control the way we live (think, feel, and choose). A more complete picture of the work of Christ will address many beliefs we have developed about God and ourselves.

We Were Created to Be in the Family of God

The following points are helpful to our understanding of why we were created and how we are to function.

- Man was created by God, Who is love, to be loved.
  ...God is love. 1 John 4:8 NASB
  Just as the Father has loved Me, I have also loved you; abide in My love. John 15:9 NASB

- Man was created in the image and likeness of God and designed to know and enjoy Him.
  Let Us make man in Our image, according to Our likeness... God created man in His own image, in the image of God He created him; male and female He created them. Genesis 1:26-27 NASB
  You will make known to me the path of life; In Your presence is fullness of joy; In Your right hand there are pleasures forever. Psalm 16:11 NASB

- Man was created to be God's child.
  See how great a love the Father has bestowed on us, that we would be called children of God; and such we are. 1 John 3:1 NASB

- Man was created to contain the very life of God and to live from Him as the Source. This is oneness.
  In that day you will know that I am in My Father, and you in Me, and I in you. John 14:20 NASB *[I ask] that they may all be one; even as You, Father, are in Me and I in You, that they also may be in Us... The glory which You have given Me I have given to them, that they may be one, just as We are one; I in them and You in Me, that they may be

Copyright 1998, 2001, 2005, 2007, 2019, 2020 Scope Ministries International, INC.

perfected in unity, so that the world may know You sent Me, and loved them, even as You have loved Me John 17:21-23 NASB

- Man was designed to live dependent upon God.
Abide in Me, and I in you. As the branch cannot bear fruit of itself unless it abides in the vine, so neither can you unless you abide in Me. I am the vine, you are the branches; he who abides in Me and I in him, he bears much fruit, for apart from Me you can do nothing. John 15:4-5 NASB

Genesis tells the story of the creation of the world and the beginning of human life. It also describes how man was deceived and chose to live life independently of God. God created man and woman and placed them in a garden paradise to live and enjoy His presence. Every day God would walk with Adam and Eve in the Garden, and He provided for every need. Adam and Eve were free to live and enjoy God's presence. The only restriction was eating from the Tree of the Knowledge of Good and Evil because it would bring death.

> *The Lord God made all sorts of trees grow up from the ground — trees that were beautiful and that produced delicious fruit. In the middle of the garden He placed the tree of life **and** the tree of the knowledge of good and evil.* Genesis 2:9 NLT

> *The Lord God placed the man in the Garden of Eden to tend and watch over it. But the Lord God warned him, "You may freely eat the fruit of every tree in the garden — except the tree of the knowledge of good and evil. If you eat its fruit, you are sure to die."* Genesis 2:15-17 NLT

In the middle of the garden, one tree held Life, the other held death. Freedom to choose is a vital part of any relationship. In order to have a relationship of love with mankind, God gave Adam and Eve the freedom to choose. When the Lord told them a certain tree would cause death, they had a will that could choose to believe His words were true or choose to believe they were false. Their actions would be based on what they chose to believe.

Satan deceived Eve by questioning God's character, word, and motives. Adam and Eve chose to believe the lie that God was not the source of life and that they could meet their own needs through the Tree of the Knowledge of Good and Evil. This lie led them to believe they could provide their own source of life; they could be their own god. When they ate from the tree, just as God had said, death came. Choosing to live independently of God is sin and this affected every aspect of their lives, causing a tragic separation in their relationship with Him.

In Adam or In Christ

Physically we are all descendants of Adam. This is what is meant when we are described as being "in Adam". We inherited separation from God and are born in a state disconnected from God. Since God is Life, to be disconnected from Him is death. The Greek word for death means to be "separated from." As a result, we are incapable of being in the living relationship He desires. This separation results in bad choices, poor judgement and behaviors in our lives. Try as we might, we cannot change our lineage through our behavior. We are all in Adam until we are born again into Christ.

Making our own decisions and depending on our own strength to live life results in our being controlled by fear, being prone to selfishness, and living in bondage to sin. Sin simply means "a loss or failure due to missing the mark." God made us to live in fellowship with Him. Without God we create our own goal or target (self-improvement program) at which we aim. In aiming for this target, we ignore what God has for us and miss the purpose for which we were created. Without a relationship we fail to know God, fail to depend upon Him, and fail to be what He created us to be.

> *Therefore, as sin came into the world through one man, and death as the result of sin, so death spread to all men, [no one being able to stop it or to escape its power] because all men sinned.* Romans 5:12 AMPC

> *And the result of God's gracious gift is very different from the result of that one man's sin. For Adam's sin led to condemnation, but God's free gift leads to our being made right with God, even though we are guilty of many sins. For the sin of this one man, Adam, caused death to rule over many. But even greater is God's wonderful grace and his gift of righteousness, for all who receive it will live in triumph over sin and death through this one man, Jesus Christ.* Romans 5:16-17 NLT

> *For since by a man came death, by a man also came the resurrection of the dead. For as **in Adam all die**, so also **in Christ all will be made alive**.* 1 Corinthians 15:21-22 NASB

This does not mean that every person accepts the gift of reconciliation provided by Christ, but it does mean that the terms of reconciliation have been met for every person in Christ. Just as the choice to be in a relationship of love and trust with God was given to Adam and Eve, so we also are given the choice of whether or not to trust our lives to Him. The receiving of this offer of reconciliation is left to each individual.

Sin kills, Christ gives life and cleanses.

Our separation from God has distorted our concept of what He is like. Therefore we formed faulty beliefs about what God is like.

The Character of God Is Redemptive

God Took It Upon Himself to Restore Our Relationship

God's redemptive actions took on the form of two main covenants expressing His heart to heal man's condition. We can see God's character in how He describes Himself in Exodus 34:6b *The Lord, the Lord God, compassionate and gracious, slow to anger, and abounding in lovingkindness and truth;*

We also see God's character in the covenants He established with mankind. Let's look at two. The Covenant made with Abraham (the Abrahamic Covenant) was initiated and carried out by God. It is eternal and is a faith-based righteousness covenant.

> *Then he [Abraham] believed in the Lord; and He reckoned it to him as righteousness.* Genesis 15:6 NASB

The second is the Mosaic Covenant referred to as the Old Covenant or the Law. God established this covenant 430 years after the Abrahamic Covenant. It was only given to the Jewish people until the coming of Christ and the establishment of the New Covenant of grace. The Law is a works-based righteousness.

> *But before faith came, we were kept in custody under the law, being shut up to the faith which was later to be revealed. Therefore the Law has become our tutor to lead us to Christ, so that we may be justified by faith.* Galatians 3:23-24 NASB

The Old and New Covenants will be discussed in more detail in an upcoming chapter.

We are deeply and unconditionally loved by God! To leave mankind in a state of irreconcilable death was not acceptable to our Creator. God tells us He is Love. (1 John 4:8) He is abounding in it! (Exodus 34:6; Psalms 103:8)

> *It was God [personally present] in Christ, reconciling and restoring the world to favor with Himself, not counting up and holding against [men] their trespasses [but canceling them], and committing to us the message of reconciliation (of the restoration to favor).* 2 Corinthians 5:19 AMPC

God's character is one of perfect, unconditional love. This means that God loves us because of Who He is, not because of how we act (rule keeping or rule breaking). We could never earn or deserve His love,

and there is nothing we can do that would cause God to stop loving us.

> *But God shows and clearly proves His [own] love for us by the fact that while we were still sinners, Christ (the Messiah, the Anointed One) died for us.* Romans 5:8 AMPC

God's love is demonstrated by His unwavering commitment to give us what we truly need through His Son, Jesus, through which He established the New Covenant. God's Word also reveals His deep emotional attachment and desire to be in a relationship with us. Understanding God's unconditional love frees us from fearing God's punishment or rejection. **We can rest in the truth that we are deeply loved.**

> *There is no fear in love [dread does not exist]. But perfect (complete, full-grown) love drives out fear, because fear involves [the expectation of divine] punishment, so the one who is afraid [of God's judgment] is not perfected in love [has not grown into a sufficient understanding of God's love]. We love, because He first loved us.* 1 John 4:18-19 AMP

God is Love and He dearly loves each of us. (Ephesians 5:2; John 17:23; 1 John 3:1) Because we were spiritually separated from God (dead), there was nothing we could do to restore our relationship with Him. But God, in His love, had a plan to take care of our sin problem and to restore us to right relationship with Him.

> *But God, being [so very] rich in mercy, because of His great and wonderful love with which He loved us, even when we were [spiritually] dead and separated from Him because of our sins, He made us [spiritually] alive together with Christ (for by His grace — His undeserved favor and mercy — you have been saved from God's judgment).* Ephesians 2:4-5 AMP

What Happened at the Cross?

Colossians tells us the certificate of our debt was nailed to the cross (Colossians 2:14). Debt is defined as something owed that a person is under obligation to repay. When we consider this in regard to sin, we realize there is a problem. Imagine trying to pay God with money, gold, or deeds. The only thing we have which is of value is the life He breathes into us.

Throughout Scripture we see blood equated with life. As strange as it sounds, blood is the currency accepted for the debt of sin, but only specific blood.

> *And according to the Law, one may almost say, all things are cleansed with blood, and without shedding of blood there is no forgiveness.* Hebrews 9:22 NASB

All of our sins (past, present, and future) were nailed to the cross.

Genesis 3:21 shows the life of an animal being taken and its skin made into garments to cover Adam and Eve. God accepted the life of an animal to cover their sins, however, this did not permanently remove them. This was temporarily acceptable until the blood of Christ was shed on the Cross. He was the only sacrificial life that could pay the debt for sin.

> *For it is impossible for the blood of bulls and goats to take away sins.*
> Hebrews 10:4 NASB

The blood of Jesus is valuable above all things in Creation. It is ample and enough for what God considers necessary to pay the full debt for the lives of every person in creation who has been born in Adam. We are completely and totally forgiven because the blood of Jesus lacked nothing and was sufficient to satisfy the holiness, righteousness, and justness of God.

> *"For this is My blood of the new covenant, which [ratifies the agreement and] is being poured out for many for the forgiveness of sins."*
> Matthew 26:28 AMPC

The night before Jesus went to the cross, He spoke the words above to His closest disciples at an event we call "the last supper." This meal was part of the remembrance of Passover where a perfect lamb was sacrificed and its blood covered the doorframes of the children of Israel who trusted in this provision from the Lord. Death passed them by and instead touched their oppressors. Jesus was expanding their understanding of this event by revealing it not only allowed Israel to become free from Egypt, but it was also a glimpse of a new agreement between Father and Son. This New Covenant would free the world from bondage to sin. It is important to understand the New Covenant began at Jesus' death, not at His birth.

> *Thus He [Jesus] does away with and annuls the first (former) order [as a means of expiating sin] so that He might inaugurate and establish the second (latter) order.* Hebrews 10:9b AMPC

> *For where there is a [last] will and testament involved, the death of the one who made it must be established, For a will and testament is valid and takes effect only at death, since it has no force or legal power as long as the one who made it is alive.* Hebrews 9:16-17 AMPC

We are completely and totally forgiven

The forgiveness we are provided by Christ's sacrifice on our behalf cleanses us entirely. Because Christ's highly valued life was given for all sin, we are not charged. God does not require payment from us on top of the full payment given by Christ on the cross. Our complete debt, past, present, and future, was paid in full by Jesus. At the time

Copyright 1998, 2001, 2005, 2007, 2019, 2020 Scope Ministries International, INC.

of the cross, our lives and the sins committed were future events. God exists outside of time and the action of Christ on the Cross resonates throughout all eternity. Therefore, it is never a matter of us doing enough to "stay" clean. Our salvation is always based on the sufficiency of what Christ has already done.

> *Much more then, having now been justified by His blood, we shall be saved from the wrath of God through Him. For if while we were enemies we were reconciled to God through the death of His Son, much more,* **having been reconciled, we shall be saved by His life.** *And not only this, but we also exult in God through our Lord Jesus Christ, through whom we have now received the reconciliation.*
> Romans 5:9-11 NASB

Read that verse again in The Message

> *Now that we are set right with God by means of this sacrificial death, the consummate blood sacrifice, there is no longer a question of being at odds with God in any way. If, when we were at our worst, we were put on friendly terms with God by the sacrificial death of his Son, now that we're at our best, just think of how our lives will expand and deepen by means of his resurrection life! Now that we have actually received this amazing friendship with God, we are no longer content to simply say it in plodding prose. We sing and shout our praises to God through Jesus, the Messiah!* Romans 5:9-11

God's salvation is a gift freely given

A gift is something that is not earned. If it is gained by performance it becomes a wage and thereby it is deserved or due. A gift is to be received. We can only receive God's gift by believing and trusting in Jesus.

> *For God did not send the Son into the world to judge the world, but that the world should be saved through Him. He who believes in Him is not judged; he who does not believe has been judged already, because he has not believed in the name of the only begotten Son of God.* John 3:17-18 NASB

> *For by grace you have been saved through faith; and that not of yourselves, it is the gift of God; not as a result of works, so that no one may boast.*
> Ephesians 2:8-9 NASB

We died with Christ and we were resurrected with Him

At the moment we trust in Christ, we who were born in Adam are put to death with Jesus. At the same moment, we are made into a new creation, being born into Christ and resurrected with Him.

> *...our old self was crucified with Him, in order that our body of sin might be done away with, so that we would no longer be slaves to sin; for he who has*

> died is freed from sin. Now if we have died with Christ, we believe that we shall also live with Him, knowing that Christ, having been raised from the dead, is never to die again; death no longer is master over Him. Romans 6:6-9 NASB

> Therefore, if anyone is in Christ, he is a new creation; old things have passed away; behold, all things have become new. 2 Corinthians 5:17 NKJV

Jesus Christ was sent to earth to reveal God's love to us, and to give His life as payment for the sins of the whole world. Again, the New Covenant mentioned by Jesus in Matthew 26:28 did not begin at His birth but at His death. Jesus experienced death as us and for us in order to reconcile our debt of sin. With the problem of sin dealt with by Christ Himself, we are now able to receive His eternal life. (1 John 4:9; Hebrews 9, Galatians 2:20)

God totally and completely accepts us!

Because of Christ's sacrifice, we can enjoy a relationship with God and can live as accepted people. God's forgiveness is complete. Knowing we have been fully cleansed and placed into Christ gives us confidence before Him and we receive His mercy and grace to help us in our time of need. (Hebrews 4:16)

> He made Him who knew no sin to be sin on our behalf, so that we might become the righteousness of God in Him. 2 Corinthians 5:21 NASB

> Moreover, I will give you a new heart and put a new spirit within you; and I will remove the heart of stone from your flesh and give you a heart of flesh. Ezekiel 36:26 NASB

We have been deeply changed within. This may not be seen outwardly as we begin the process of understanding who we now are in Christ, but it is true just the same. God accepts us as we are and where we are, knowing we are perfected and secure in His Son. (Hebrews 10:14)

God's acceptance does not mean He approves of the wrong things we do. He will reveal to us that those behaviors are like old clothes that do not fit anymore. We have been clothed in the righteousness of Jesus. As we begin to understand and affirm our new identity, our beliefs about God, ourselves, life and others will change.

> ... and affirm together with the Lord, that you walk no longer just as the Gentiles also walk, in the futility of their mind, being darkened in their understanding, excluded from the life of God because of the ignorance that is in them, because of the hardness of their heart; Ephesians 4:18-19 NASB

Copyright 1998, 2001, 2005, 2007, 2019, 2020 Scope Ministries International, INC.

> *in reference to your former manner of life, you lay aside the old self, which is being corrupted in accordance with the lusts of deceit, and that you be renewed in the spirit of your mind, and put on the new self, which in the likeness of God has been created in righteousness and holiness of the truth.*
> Ephesians 4:22-24 NASB

During this process of renewing our minds, God does not shake His head in disappointment, wondering how many more times we will mess up before we finally get it right. God is fully aware of each step we will take on our journey and even knew our tracks before Jesus went to the cross. We are the only ones surprised by our choices. Long before we chose to follow God, He chose us and He has promised He will not leave us to navigate alone. (Hebrews 13:5) God receives us to Himself with pleasure and responds to us in kindness. We are entirely accepted because He is good, kind, and knows all.

We have been given eternal life

"Jesus did not come to make bad people good. He came to make dead people alive." Quote attributed to C.S. Lewis.

> *And you were dead in your trespasses and sins, in which you formerly walked according to the course of this world, according to the prince of the power of the air, of the spirit that is now working in the sons of disobedience… But God, being rich in mercy, because of His great love with which He loved us, even when we were dead in our transgressions, made us alive together with Christ.* Ephesians 2:1, 4-5 NASB

Our old dead self is put to death with Christ, we are buried with Him and raised back to life in Him. We are given a new spirit that is in His likeness. God gives Jesus' Eternal Life to all who believe in His Son and receive Him as their personal Savior.

Eternal Life is God's divine life given to us now. This means we can experientially know God now, in the midst of whatever problems we may face.

> *This is eternal life, that they may know You, the only true God, and Jesus Christ whom You have sent.*
> John 17:3 NASB

We become capable of experiencing abundant life because Holy Spirit lives in us

God's eternal, Holy Spirit indwells us, so we can know and enjoy an intimate relationship with God. Eternal Life is not just living forever, but it is the presence of God in us now. We are now, and will be forever, in the

The very essence of the Gospel is not to get man into Heaven, but to get God into man!

loving presence of God. Abundant life is joy and satisfaction in God, regardless of outward circumstances. We do not earn abundant life by our performance. It is produced in us by the Holy Spirit.

> *I came that they may have life, and have it abundantly.* John 10:10b NASB

> *For we are the temple of the living God; just as God said, "I will dwell in them and walk among them; And I will be their God, and they shall be My people."* 2 Corinthians 6:16 NASB

> *I will put My Spirit within you and cause you to walk in My statutes, and you will be careful to observe My ordinances.* Ezekiel 36:27 NASB

> *But if the Spirit of Him who raised Jesus from the dead dwells in you, He who raised Christ Jesus from the dead will also give life to your mortal bodies through His Spirit who dwells in you.* Romans 8:11 NASB

God lives through us by His Holy Spirit

Holy Spirit reveals God's unconditional love to us. As this revelation occurs, Holy Spirit reproduces His character within us. This character produces fruit and is the very nature of God living through His children. We often believe that the fruit of the Spirit is something we are responsible to generate through discipline and willpower. We simply cannot do this. We do not produce His character by our behavior. The fruit of the Spirit is God expressing Himself as He lives through us.

> *But the fruit of the [Holy] Spirit [the work which His presence within accomplishes] is love, joy (gladness), peace, patience (an even temper, forbearance), kindness, goodness (benevolence), faithfulness, gentleness (meekness, humility), self-control (self- restraint, continence).* Galatians 5:22-23a AMP

> *I am crucified with Christ: nevertheless I live; yet not I, but Christ liveth in me: and the life which I now live in the flesh I live by the faith of the Son of God, who loved me, and gave Himself for me.* Galatians 2:20 KJV

The work of Christ on the Cross is often taught to be forgiveness of our sins. Being forgiven is truly good and something every person born in Adam is desperately in need of. However, so much more was accomplished on the Cross. When Jesus removes sin, He can then begin to live through us.

Distortion Of The Truth Leads to Problems

Whenever we misunderstand the Good News of the Gospel, we view our relationship with God and the Christian life in a distorted way. The very essence of the Gospel is not to get man into Heaven, but to get God into man!

Viewing salvation as merely "fire insurance" or a free ticket to Heaven can result in our:
- Continuing to live independently of God

Copyright 1998, 2001, 2005, 2007, 2019, 2020 Scope Ministries International, INC.

- Neglecting the relationship He wants us to enjoy now
- Looking to life's circumstances and others for our happiness

Most Christians define the Gospel as God's effort to get man into Heaven. However, salvation is more than forgiveness and going to Heaven someday. If we simply try to get into Heaven, we miss the whole point of knowing God as He lives in us.

Viewing God's forgiveness as incomplete or conditional results in our:

- Believing Jesus died only for the sins we committed before we became a Christian
- Believing we have to ask for forgiveness before we are forgiven
- Believing God is angry with us and holding our sins against us
- Viewing ourselves as being on parole instead of fully pardoned
- Feeling emotional guilt and fearing punishment, which creates distance in our relationship with God
- Continually asking God for forgiveness but never experiencing the peace His total forgiveness brings

Believing we are saved primarily to serve God leads to:

- Trying to do things for God in order to earn His acceptance
- Living from our own strength and ability rather than depending on the power of the Holy Spirit
- Believing God is more interested in our behavior than in a relationship with us
- Being spiritually proud based on our performance, abilities, or sacrifice

Believing the Truth Transforms Our Lives

Our purpose and the meaning we give to life will change

Increasingly, our purpose will be to enjoy a love relationship with God. Rather than always trying to avoid pain, we will begin to see problems as opportunities to know God experientially.

> *Yes, furthermore, I count everything as loss compared to the surpassing value of knowing Christ Jesus my Lord and progressively becoming more deeply and intimately acquainted with Him.* Philippians 3:8-10 paraphrase

The way we view God and respond to Him will change

The Gospel demonstrates the beauty of God's grace and unconditional love for us. The more we believe God's love, the more easily we will trust Him in

We can continue to feel separated from God if we don't believe we are forgiven, loved, and accepted by God.

the midst of life's problems. We will draw near to Him in times of trouble and failure.

> *You will make known to me the path of life; In Your presence is fullness of joy; In Your right hand there are pleasures forever.* Psalm 16:11 NASB

> *As for the rich in this world, charge them not to be proud and arrogant and contemptuous of others, nor to set their hopes on uncertain riches, but on God, Who richly and ceaselessly provides us with everything for [our] enjoyment.* 1 Timothy 6:17 AMP

The way we view ourselves and how we relate to others will change

Believing this Good News causes us to see ourselves as God's dearly loved children, not just forgiven sinners. We will begin to relate to others the way God relates to us. We will forgive, love, and accept others in the same way and to the same degree we believe God has forgiven, loved, and accepted us.

> *Therefore, accept one another, just as Christ also accepted us to the glory of God.* Romans 15:7 NASB

> *Be kind to one another, tender-hearted, forgiving each other, just as God in Christ also has forgiven you.* Ephesians 4:32 NASB

> *So, as those who have been chosen of God, holy and beloved, put on a heart of compassion, kindness, humility, gentleness and patience; bearing with one another, and forgiving each other, whoever has a complaint against anyone; just as the Lord forgave you, so also should you.* Colossians 3:12-13 NASB

Receiving Christ into our life is a one-time decision. However, believing the Good News is an ongoing one. Daily, we put our confidence in the work of Jesus Christ and continue believing and acting on the things that are now true about us. This involves believing that Christ's death on the cross guarantees our total forgiveness and enables us to enjoy an intimate love relationship with God.

Summary:

1. We were created to be in the family of God

2. God took it upon Himself to restore our relationship

3. We are completely and totally forgiven

4. We have been given Eternal Life

5. God lives through us by His Holy Spirit

Jesus gave His life for us, so He can give His life to us, so He can live His life in us, so He could reveal His life through us.

A Life Transformed continued…

I started studying the Bible a couple of times a week with a friend, and the truth about God and what He thinks about me helped ease my fears. I realized that God wants a relationship with me, not performance from me. I learned that He wouldn't condemn me or reprimand me. I knew that God changes lives, but I wasn't sure that He would change mine. I decided to give Him a try, and I accepted Christ's forgiveness and invited Him to take control of my life.

As I believed and received the truth of God's unconditional love and forgiveness, the feelings of abandonment and rejection began to diminish. I was freed from the thoughts that tormented me to contemplate suicide and despair. My whole perspective has changed. I've got a lot more than I had, but it's not stuff. I have confidence because I don't have to worry about making the wrong choice. I know I have Someone to guide me though all my problems.

Understanding God's approval is the key to everything. People told me before that I'm worthy and OK, but I didn't believe them. Now I know it's true because I have His words on who I am. Otherwise, I would still be believing the lie that there is something wrong with me. I would still be beating myself up all the time about what I've done. Now I don't consider my past failures because I'm focused on the future God has for me.

I used to seclude myself because I was afraid of rejection, and people around me avoided me because they thought I looked angry all the time. Now I am at ease with myself and that allows me to go out and be a part of this world. I have gained many new friends, and people actually talk to me because I don't scare them anymore.

My attitude towards work has also changed. At my job, now I enjoy accomplishing good work and relating to others to achieve a common goal. Daily chores and necessities are enjoyable because I focus on enjoying the work and not worrying about the results.

Now I have a present life instead of past failures and future fears. I discovered this new life from God's truth, and I desire to live and grow in it. I know that it is a Spirit-led journey and that God in me will make me able to live it.

Jeff - Printing Supervisor

The Truth About The Cross - Day One

Recognize your present view of God and how this has affected your understanding of the finished work of the Cross.

1. Until now, what has been your understanding of Salvation?

2. Read the lesson and then write a definition of the Truth About the Cross.

3. Think of a recent time when you were very disappointed with your behavior, and with this in mind, complete the following statements:

    When God thinks about me, He is . . .

    God expects me to . . .

    God is angry with me when I . . .

    God would be more pleased with me if I . . .

    The one thing that frightens me most about God is . . .

4. Based on your answers from question 3, write a description of how you think God views you when you fail.

> Example: "When God thinks about me, He gets angry." This might reveal a belief that God has not forgiven you.

5. What misunderstanding of the Good News is reflected by your answers in questions 3 and 4?

> Example: Believing God is unforgiving reveals a misunderstanding of God's total forgiveness of your sins.

6. Your answers may show how your concept of God has been distorted.. Look back at this lesson and find a Scripture that challenges your distorted view of God and salvation. Based on this verse, write a prayer to God expressing thanks for His completed work on the Cross.

The Truth About The Cross - Day Two

Understand how God responds to you when you sin.

1. Read John 8:3-11, observing the woman's behavior and Jesus' response.

    a. What was the woman's behavior?

    b. What was Jesus' response to her?

2. Read Luke 15:11-24. The father in this parable represents God, and the two sons represent two types of people.

    a. What was the younger son's behavior?

    b. What was the father's response to the younger son?

    c. What did the son do to get his father's forgiveness?

3. Based on the above examples, how does God respond to you when you sin?

4. Besides forgiving, what else is revealed about God's character in the above passages?

5. How would viewing God this way affect the way you relate to Him in your present situation?

6. Write a prayer expressing to God your desire to experience Him in this way.

The Truth About The Cross - Day Three

Understand more accurately from Scripture the total forgiveness God extends to you.

Knowing and enjoying God's forgiveness is imperative to a healthy Christian life. What incredible joy it brings when we realize what God has done about our sin. We can now come confidently into His presence with the assurance that our sins are not only forgiven—but forgotten! Based on Hebrews 10, God not only forgives, but chooses to forget our sins and transgressions. What this means is that God will never throw them back in our faces.

1. What do you feel God is still holding against you?

2. Read each verse below and write down what God is telling you personally about His forgiveness and what you have been given in Christ.

> *You were dead in sins, and your sinful desires were not yet cut away. Then He gave you a share in the very life of Christ, for He forgave all your sins, and blotted out the charges proved against you, the list of his commandments which you had not obeyed. He took this list of sins and destroyed it by nailing it to Christ's cross.* Colossians 2:13-14 LB

> *The Lord your God is in the midst of you, a Mighty One, a Savior [Who saves]! He will rejoice over you with joy . . . and in His love He will be silent and make no mention [of past sins, or even recall them]; He will exalt over you with singing.* Zephaniah 3:17 AMPC

> *As far as the east is from the west, so far has He removed our transgressions from us.*
> Psalm 103:12 NASB

I, even I, am He Who blots out and cancels your transgressions, for My own sake, and I will not remember your sins. Isaiah 43:25 AMPC

Therefore there is now no condemnation for those who are in Christ Jesus. For the law of the Spirit of life in Christ Jesus has set you free from the law of sin and of death. Romans 8:1-2 NASB

3. Based on these verses, how many of your sins has God forgiven? Remember, Jesus died for all the sins of the whole world. That means He has already paid for all your future sins as well.

4. Write a note to God thanking Him for His complete forgiveness.

The Truth About The Cross - Day Four

Understand more fully the free gift of eternal life.

1. When you became a Christian, what did you receive?

> *Truly, truly, I say to you, he who hears My word, and believes Him who sent Me, has eternal life, and does not come into judgment, but has passed out of death into life.* John 5:24 NASB

2. Read that verse in the Amplified version below. How and when does one receive eternal life?

> *I assure you, most solemnly I tell you, the person whose ears are open to My words [who listens to My message] and believes and trusts in and clings to and relies on Him Who sent Me has (possesses now) eternal life. And he does not come into judgment [does not incur sentence of judgment, will not come under condemnation], but he has already passed over out of death into life.* John 5:24 AMPC

Often we think of eternal life as merely living forever after death (future) instead of something we receive at salvation and can experience now.

The word "life" is the Greek word zoe which refers to the principle of life in the spirit and soul (as opposed to life in the body). Zoe represents the highest and best, which Christ is and which He gives to those who believe in Him. It is God's quality of life, which is given to His children. We can better experience zoe, God's quality of life, the more we know, perceive, recognize, become acquainted with, and understand God as He really is.

3. Remembering the definition of zoe, read the following verses. Below each one write your observations concerning "eternal life."

> *In order that everyone who believes in Him [who cleaves to Him, trusts Him, and relies on Him] may not perish, but have eternal life and [actually] live forever! For God so greatly loved and dearly prized the world, that He [even] gave up His only begotten (unique) Son, so that whoever believes in (trusts in, clings to, relies on) Him shall not perish (come to destruction, be lost) but have eternal (everlasting) life.* John 3:15-16 AMPC

The thief (Satan) comes only in order to steal and kill and destroy. I (Jesus) came that they may have and enjoy life, and have it in abundance (to the full, till it overflows). John 10:10 AMPC

For this is My Father's will and His purpose, that everyone who sees the Son and believes in and cleaves to and trusts in and relies on Him should have eternal life, and I will raise Him up [from the dead] at the last day. I assure you, most solemnly I tell you, he who believes in Me [who adheres to, trusts in, relies on and has faith in Me] has (now possesses) eternal life. John 6:40,47 AMPC

And this is eternal life: [it means] to know (to perceive, recognize, become acquainted with, and understand) You, the only true and real God, and [likewise] to know Him, Jesus [as the] Christ (the Anointed One, the Messiah), Whom You have sent. John 17:3 AMPC

I write this to you who believe in (adhere to, trust in, and rely on) the name of the Son of God [in the peculiar services and blessings conferred by Him on men], so that you may know [with settled and absolute knowledge] that you [already] have life, yes, eternal life.. 1 John 5:13 AMPC

4. What new understanding do these verses give you concerning "eternal life"?

5. God is eternal life, the source of all life. Apart from Him there is no real life. He has chosen to give His life to those who will believe, and who receive Jesus' offer of forgiveness and eternal life. If you have never personally received Jesus as your life you may do this now by simply taking Him at His word and accepting the gift of His life.

But to as many as did receive and welcome Him, He gave the authority (power, privilege, right) to become the children of God, that is, to those who believe in (adhere to, trust in, and rely on) His name. John 1:12 AMPC

The Truth About The Cross - Day Five

Learn how salvation applies to your daily life.

1. Eternal life is not just longevity of life but God's quality of life that is to be experienced now, in the midst of life's problems. How does this give you hope in your situation?

2. How would believing God has completely forgiven you, unconditionally loves you, and totally accepts you change the way you relate to God?

3. According to the following verse answer this question, "Are we saved by the death of Christ or Are we saved by the life of Christ?

> *For if while we were enemies we were reconciled to God through the death of His Son, much more, having been reconciled, we shall be saved by His life (in us).* Romans 5:10 NASB

> Our salvation is not merely an event in our past, but it is to be our ongoing daily experience. As we call upon Jesus in the midst of life's problem, His life is revealed.

4. Read the following verses and under each one write, in your own words, God's promise to you in your present situation.

> *For I am persuaded beyond doubt (am sure) that neither death nor life, nor angels nor principalities, nor things impending and threatening nor things to come, nor powers, nor height nor depth, nor anything else in all creation will be able to separate us from the love of God which is in Christ Jesus our Lord.* Romans 8:38-39 AMPC

> Example: There is nothing from my past or in my present or in my future that will cause God to stop loving me.

For He [God] Himself has said, I will not in any way fail you nor give you up nor leave you without support. [I will] not, [I will] not, [I will] not in any degree leave you helpless nor forsake nor let [you] down (relax My hold on you)! [Assuredly not!] Hebrews 13:5b AMPC

Do not fear, for I am with you; do not anxiously look about you, for I am your God. I will strengthen you, surely I will help you, surely I will uphold you with My righteous right hand. Isaiah 41:10 NASB

[Not in your own strength] for it is God Who is all the while effectually at work in you [energizing and creating in you the power and desire], both to will and to work for His good pleasure and satisfaction and delight. Philippians 2:13 AMPC

And I am convinced and sure of this very thing, that He Who began a good work in you will continue until the day of Jesus Christ [right up to the time of His return], developing [that good work] and perfecting and bringing it to full completion in you. Philippians 1:6 AMPC

5. According to what God has promised, is there any reason for you not to have hope? Why or why not?

6. Spend some time thanking God for His promises to you.

The Truth About The Cross - Lesson Two
Summary Page

1. What impacted you the most in examining the meaning and application of salvation?

2. How do you feel God responds to you when you fail in some way?

3. How does knowing God totally forgives you affect your personal walk with Him?

4. What is the difference between everlasting life and eternal life?

5. How would you describe the difference between God loving you, accepting you and seeking you? Which one intrigues you?

Appendix
The Good News

Good News Masquerading as Bad News

Gen 2:17	For in the day that you eat of it you shall surely die
John 3:18	Whoever does not believe is condemned already
Rom 3:10-12	No one does good, not even one (Ps 14:4; 53:3)
Rom 3:23	All have sinned and fall short of the glory of God
Rom 6:23	The wages of sin is death
Eph 2:1, 5	You were dead in your trespasses and sins
Eph 2:3	Were by nature children of wrath
Eph 2:12	Separated from Christ
Col 1:21	And you, who once were alienated and hostile in mind
Col 2:13	You who were dead in your trespasses

The Initiator

Jer 31:31-34	Seven "I will" statements (Heb 8:10; 10:16)
Jer 32:39-40	A bunch of "I will" statements (contrast with the flesh's "I will" in Is 14:13-14)
Eze 36:26-27	A bunch of "I will" statements
Luke 15	Parables of the searching shepherd / searching woman / searching father looking for what was lost
John 6:44	No one can come to me unless the Father who sent me draws him.
John 15:16	You did not choose me, but I chose you
Rom 1:6	Called to belong to Jesus Christ
Rom 1:7	Loved by God and called to be saints
Rom 5:8	While we were still sinners, Christ died for us
2 Cor 5:18	God, who through Christ reconciled us to himself
Eph 1:4	He chose us in him before the creation of the world
Eph 2:4-5a	But God, being rich in mercy … made us alive together with Christ
Col 1:13	He has delivered us from the domain of darkness and transferred us to the kingdom his beloved son
Col 2:14	Canceling the record of debt that stood against us with its legal demands
1 John 3:1	See what love the Father has given us, that we should be called children of God
1 John 4:9	God sent his only Son into the world, so that we might live through him
1 John 4:10	This is love, not that we have loved God, but that he loved us
1 John 4:19	We love him because he first loved us.
Rev 1:5b-6	To him who loved us and has freed us from our sins by his blood (Ps 136:23-24)

The Gift of Life

John 10:28a	I gave them eternal life
John 14:6	I am the way, the truth, and the life
Rom 3:24	Are justified by his grace as a gift
Rom 6:23	The free gift of God is eternal life in Christ Jesus
Eph 2:5b	By grace you have been saved
Eph 2:8	By grace you have been saved through faith
Col 1:12	The Father, who has qualified you to share in the inheritance of the saints
Col 2:13	You who were dead, God made alive
Col 2:13	Having forgiven us all our trespasses
Rev 5:9b	For you were slain and by your blood you ransomed people for God

Copyright 1998, 2001, 2005, 2007, 2019, 2020 Scope Ministries International, INC.

Assurance of Salvation – Past, Present, and Future

John 10:28b	No one will snatch them out of my hand
Rom 6:18,22	Having been set free from sin
Eph 2:8	It is the gift of God, not the result of works
Heb 10:10	We have been sanctified through the offering of the body of Christ once for all
1 John 1:9	He will forgive us our sins and purify us from all unrighteousness
1 John 2:2	He is the propitiation for our sins
1 John 2:12	Your sins are forgiven for his name's sake
1 John 3:5	He appeared in order to take away sins

I didn't gain my salvation by my good performance,
therefore I cannot lose my salvation by my poor performance.

What HAS Been Done By God In My Life

Rom 5:1	We have been justified by faith
Rom 5:1	We have peace with God
Rom 5:5	God's love has been poured into our hearts through the Holy Spirit
Rom 5:5	The Holy Spirit who has been given to us
Rom 6:2	We who died to sin
Rom 6:3	Were baptized into his death
Rom 6:4	We were buried therefore with him
Rom 6:5	We have been united with him
Rom 6:6	Our old self was crucified with him
Rom 6:8	We have died with Christ (2 Cor 5:14)
Rom 6:17	Have become obedient from the heart
Rom 6:18	Having been set free from sin
Rom 6:22	Have been set free from sin
Rom 6:22	Have become slaves to God
1 Cor 6:15	Your bodies are members of Christ
2 Cor 5:17	Are a new creation
2 Cor 5:20	We are ambassadors of Christ
Eph 1:3	Who has blessed us in Christ with every spiritual blessing
Eph 1:13	were sealed with the promised Holy Spirit
Eph 2:22	In him you also are being built together into a dwelling place for God by the Spirit
Phil 3:12	Christ Jesus has made me his own
Col 2:6	We received Christ Jesus the Lord
Col 2:10	You have been filled in him
Col 2:11	You were circumcised with a circumcision made without hands
Col 2:12	Buried with him in baptism
Col 2:12	You were also raised with him
Col 2:13	God made alive together with him
Col 2:13	having forgiven us all our trespasses

Col 2:20	You died to the elemental spirits of the world
Col 3:1	You have been raised with Christ
Col 3:3	You have died
Col 3:3	Your life is hidden in Christ
Heb 10:16	I will put my laws on their hearts and write them on their minds (Jer 31:33)
1 John 2:20	You have been anointed by the Holy One
1 John 5:11	God gave us eternal life

How a Believer Has Changed

John 14:20	I am in my Father, and you in me, and I in you
John 14:23	We will make our home in him
John 15:11	That my joy may be in you, and that your joy may be full
John 16:13	When the Holy Spirit comes, he will guide you into all truth
Rom 1:6	Called to belong to Jesus Christ
Rom 1:7	Called to be saints
Rom 8:14	Are sons of God
Rom 8:16	We are children of God
1 Cor 1:2	Called to be saints
2 Cor 5:17	We are a new creation
2 Cor 5:21	We might become the righteousness of God
Gal 2:20	Christ lives in me
Eph 1:1	(They are) saints
Eph 1:13	Were sealed with the promised Holy Spirit
Eph 2:6	Raised us up with him and seated us in the heavenly places in Christ Jesus
Col 3:1	You have been raised with Christ
1 John 2:20	You have been anointed by the Holy One and you have all knowledge
1 John 2:26	The anointing that you received from him abides in you
1 John 3:1	That we should be called children of God; and so we are
1 John 3:2	We are God's children
1 John 3:6	No one who abides in him keeps on sinning
1 John 4:4	He who is in you is greater than he who is in the world

How God Continues Conforming Us to the Image of Jesus

Ps 138:8	The LORD will fulfill his purpose for me
Matt 4:19	I will make you fishers of men
John 10:10	I came that they may have life and have it abundantly
John 14:16-17	I will ask the Father and he will give you another Helper to be with you forever
John 15:5	He will bear much fruit
John 15:16	I chose you and appointed you that you should go and bear much fruit
Rom 8:29	For those he foreknew he also predestined to be conformed to the image of his Son
2 Cor 3:18	Are being transformed into the same image
2 Cor 5:18	Gave us the ministry of reconciliation
Eph 2:10	We are his workmanship
Phil 1:6	He who began a good work in you will bring it to completion
Phil 2:13	It is God who works in you, both to will and to work for his good pleasure
Heb 10:14	He has perfected for all time those who are being sanctified
Heb 13:21	Equip you with everything good that you may do his will, working in us that which is pleasing in his sight

1 John 3:1   When he appears, we shall be like him
Jude 24   Now to him who is able and willing to keep you from falling and to present before his glorious presence without fault and with great joy

Implications of an Economy of Grace
Rom 3:27   Then what becomes of boasting? It is excluded.
Eph 2:8   This is not of your own doing, it is the gift of God
Eph 2:9   Not as a result of works, so that no one may boast (Rom 4:2)

Examples of the Good News
Rom 4:9   Faith was counted to Abraham as righteousness (Gen 15:6)
Rom 4:22   His faith was counted to him as righteousness (Gen 15:6)

The Logic of Grace
The degree to which I depend upon grace for my salvation:
Is my degree of assurance. I cannot lose something that I didn't earn in the first place.
Is the degree to which I will praise God.
Is the degree to which I do not feel the need to boast about my accomplishments.

The degree to which I depend upon grace for my sanctification:
Is the degree to which I will be conformed to the likeness of Jesus
Is the degree to which I will depend upon God in my daily life.

The Logic of Works
The degree to which I feel responsible for my salvation:
Is the degree to which I will feel that I can lose my salvation.
If I earned it by doing something good, then I can lose it be doing something bad
Is the degree to which I will not praise God.
I do not praise another person for something that I have accomplished
Is the degree to which I will feel the need to boast about my accomplishments.

The degree to which I feel responsible for my sanctification:
Is the degree to which I will fail.
Is the degree to which I will be disappointed in myself.
Is the degree to which I will feel that God is disappointed in me.
Is the degree to which I will drift away from God.
It is no fun to be around people that remind us of our failures, and we all fall short.

The extent to which I think that I deserve God's goodness is the extent to which I will struggle with:
    Grace   Grace and wages cannot go together
    Failure I am now responsible for maintaining this attribute that makes me worthy of God's love. When I fail, God will stop loving me. I might even lose my salvation.

The Short Version of the Good News
It is not us seeking or finding God, but rather God being the Initiator:
while we were still sinners, Christ died for us (Romans 5:8)

The Truth About Your New Identity

When someone becomes a Christian he becomes a brand new person inside. He is not the same any more. A new life has begun! 2 Corinthians 5:17 LB

Lesson Three

A Life Transformed

Much of my life I performed to try to gain the acceptance from people — from my family, from my friends, and especially from God. I believed that to be liked and respected, I had to accomplish something to prove myself worthy of their approval.

Many of my childhood experiences developed this belief. Whenever I showed my report card to my parents they didn't say, "Good job for the A's and B's," but "Why the C's? Can't you do any better than that?" I also noticed that the athletes were always the popular people at school. They were asked to parties. They were recognized for their accomplishments. Everyone wanted to be with them. Because I was never athletic, I felt unaccepted and not worthy of attention from my peers.

I carried this false belief into my relationship with God. Who got the recognition in church? Usually they were the overseas missionary, the one with perfect church attendance for 100 years, and the person who gave a lot of money. My definition of a saint was someone who taught Sunday School for 30 years! I hadn't accomplished these things, so I knew I wasn't important there either.

I believed that I had to work to get God's approval by having a quiet time every morning, memorizing two Bible verses every week, and witnessing to anyone and everyone — especially to anyone sitting next to me on an airplane! But as much as I tried to please God, there was always something more that I should have done.

Maybe I should have joined the church choir.

to be continued...

The Truth About Your New Identity
Lesson Three

The Truth of Your New Identity

As we saw in Lesson Two, the Truth About God, our relationship with our Heavenly Father is greatly impacted by what we believe to be true about Him. When we see His goodness and love toward us, we find it easier to trust Him in all areas of our lives. In this lesson we explore how we are made in His image and why that matters in how we perceive ourselves and how we relate to God our Father. We will see how a life exchange has been made. We are no longer in Adam, but in Christ. We have been given a new identity, which we will explore in this lesson.

> *"To those who have obtained like precious faith with us by the righteousness of our God and Savior Jesus Christ. Grace and peace be multiplied to you in the knowledge of God and of Jesus our Lord. As His divine power has given to us all things that pertain to life and godliness, through the knowledge of Him who called us by glory and virtue. By which have been given to us exceedingly great and precious promises, that through these you may be* **partakers of the divine nature,** *having escaped the corruption that is in the world through lust." 2 Peter 1:1-4* NKJV

Our experiences in this fallen world form the beliefs we hold. We believe what the world tells us about ourselves despite who God says we are as His Children. This lesson will enable us to recognize our faulty beliefs about ourselves which contradict who God has made us to be in Christ.

We were created in the image of God

The way we were designed by God corresponds to His purpose in creating us. God is love. (1 John 4:8) We were created by Love and created for love; both to receive love from Him and to express His love to others. We were created in His image to live by His life, and to express His character.

> *"So God created man in His own image, in the image and likeness of God He created him; male and female He created them."*
> Genesis 1:27 Amplified

> *"For whom He foreknew, He also predestined to be conformed to the image of His Son, that He might be the firstborn among many brethren."*
> Romans 8:29 NKJV

Copyright 1998, 2001, 2005, 2007, 2019, 2020 Scope Ministries International, INC.

We Are Made of Three Basic Parts: Spirit, Soul and Body

God created us complete, whole beings. Scripture refers to us as *spirit, soul, and body* to reveal the parts of the whole and to teach us how we are to function within that whole.

> *Then the Lord God formed man from the dust of the ground [body] and breathed into his nostrils the breath or spirit of life [spirit], and the man became a living being [soul].* Genesis 2:7 AMP

Our bodies were formed from the earth, so we could relate to the physical world. He created us a living soul to relate to both the visible, physical world, and the invisible, spiritual world. It is by our human spirit we relate to Him.

> *And may the God of peace Himself sanctify you through and through;...and may your spirit and soul and body be preserved sound and complete [and found] blameless at the coming of our Lord Jesus Christ [the Messiah].* 1 Thessalonians 5:23 AMP

We can use an analogy of a tree to help us understand our three-part nature

A tree has three main parts: leaves, trunk, and roots. Three parts make a whole tree. This illustrates how our three parts (body, soul, and spirit) combine to make us a whole person.

Like the leaves of the tree, our body is the most visible and changeable aspect of who we are. Our body has physical needs such as nourishment, exercise, and rest. Our body is our means of "doing" and of relating to the world through our five senses: taste, touch, smell, sight and sound. Our body is temporal (earthly) and visible.

Just as the trunk gives the tree its unique form, so the soul gives us our unique personality. Our soul has needs; to be loved, accepted, and found significant. Our soul includes our mind allowing us to know God; our emotions so we may enjoy God; and our will to choose and trust God. Our soul expresses our thoughts, feelings, and choices. It is our means of relating to others. Our soul is eternal yet visible through our choices.

The roots of a tree are not visible; however, they are the most important aspect of the tree, drawing the nutrients for life into the tree. A tree without roots cannot survive. In the same way, a body without a spirit is dead. The Spirit gives us life and determines our identity. Our spirits were made to receive life (nutrients) from God. The spirit is our means of knowing and responding to God, who is Spirit. Our human spirit is eternal and invisible.

Being created in God's image means we are a three-part creation as He is a three part God.

Copyright 1998, 2001, 2005, 2007, 2019, 2020 Scope Ministries International, INC.

At Creation

Leaves: Body had capaciy for immortality
Obedient to God's ways

Trunk: Mind dependent on spirit for truth
Will is harmony with self and others
Emotions expressed God's character

Roots: Spirit alive and relating to God
Desired to please God
Was God's image bearer

Unbelief - The Root of Sin

Man's separation from God affected all three parts of his nature

Unbelief started in the Garden of Eden. Unbelief was possible for man through the exercise of their free will given to them by God. Before the first bite of fruit from the forbidden tree could be taken, an exchange was made, a lie for the truth. The truth of God's character and Adam and Eve's God-given identity were stolen through cunning deception.

The first couple chose the lie rather than the truth. Deception tricked them into believing God lied to them and caused them to believe there was more they could experience and achieve than what God had given them. They believed God was withholding good from them and He was not enough for life and godliness. Rather than live dependent upon God, man made the choice to live independently of God, believing they could be their own "god."

> "Now the serpent was more cunning than any beast of the field which the LORD God had made. And he said to the woman, Has God indeed said, 'You shall not eat of every tree of the garden?'" *Genesis 3:1 NKJV*

> "For God knows that in the day you eat of it your eyes will be opened, and you will be like God, knowing good and evil." *Genesis 3:5 NKJV*

Believing the lie separated man from God. The human spirit could no longer receive revelation from God; therefore, man began to determine truth for himself in his soul. Void of truth as God defines it, man's mind became darkened, lacking spiritual understanding and believing lies as truth. Because of man's deceived mind, his will became rebellious,

and his emotions became controlling. Man's body became an instrument of sin and man began to die.

> *"For all have sinned and fallen short of the glory of God."* Romans 3:23 NASB

> *"For since the creation of the world His invisible attributes are clearly seen, being understood by the things that are made, even His eternal power and Godhead so that they are without excuse. Because, although they knew God, they did not glorify Him as God, nor were thankful, but became futile in their thoughts and their foolish hearts were darkened. Professing to be wise, they became fools. They exchanged the truth of God for a lie, and worshipped and served the creature rather than the Creator, who is blessed forever. Amen."* Romans 1:20-22, 25 NKJV

Believing lies as truth, man lived to gratify himself and to meet his own needs from the only resources left to him. Man became attracted to things that pleased his senses and rejected those things that did not. Having his focus on his life (on himself), man became selfish and prone to sinful behavior. This is our condition apart from God; self-serving and enslaved to sin.

> *"And just as they did not see fit to acknowledge God any longer, God gave them over to a depraved mind, to do those things which are not proper, being filled with all unrighteousness, . . . and, although they know the ordinance of God, that those who practice such things are worthy of death, they not only do the same, but also give hearty approval to those who practice them."* Romans 1:28-29a, 32 NAS

At Separation

Body
Mortal, weakend and dying
Disobedient to God's way

Soul
Mind darkened, beliefs corrupted
Will enslaved to sin, self-serving
Emotions controlling

Spirit
Spirit dead to God, alive to sin
Desired to please self
Child of Satan

Jesus Christ Restores God's Image in Us

The cross of Christ accomplished more than the forgiveness of our sins. Likewise the cross was our instrument of death. We were co-crucified with Christ. We were placed into Christ's death and when He died, we died. Additionally, when we died with Christ, our old man died. When we were buried with Him, our old identity was buried with Him. In the grave, Christ made us alive with Him in new life. He gave us life - His life. When Christ rose from the grave, we rose with Him into His life and righteousness within us.

> *Or do you not know that as many of us as were baptized into Christ Jesus were baptized into His death? Therefore, we were buried with Him through baptism into death, that just as Christ was raised from the dead by the glory of the Father, even so we also should walk in newness of life. For if we have been united together in the likeness of His death, certainly we also shall be in the likeness of His resurrection, knowing this, that our old man was crucified with Him, that the body of sin might be done away with, that we should no longer be slaves of sin. For he who has died has been freed from sin. Now if we died with Christ, we believe that we shall also live with Him."* Romans 6:2-8 NKJV

> *"Therefore, if anyone is in Christ, he is a new creation; old things have passed away; behold, all things have become new. For He made Him who knew no sin to be sin for us, that we might become the righteousness of God in Him."* 2 Corinthians 5:17, 21 NKJV

> *"I am crucified with Christ: nevertheless I live; yet not I, but Christ liveth in me: and the life which I now live in the flesh I live by the faith of the Son of God, who loved me, and gave himself for me."* Galatians 2:20 KJV

Christ gave us a brand new identity

As spirit-born children of God, we have received a new nature and new identity. We are no longer who we think we are. God does not see us according to our deeds or performance but according to His deeds and His performance. Our spirit is now one with His Spirit. God's word describes how God now sees us. As God's new creations bearing His life we are:

- totally and completely forgiven (Ephesians 1:7; Colossians 2:13-14)
- completely acceptable and accepted (Romans 15:7; Ephesians 1:4)
- absolutely righteous (Ephesians 4:24; 2 Corinthians 5:21)
- perfect in Christ (Hebrews 10:14)

Your New Identity

- holy and blameless (Colossians 1:22)
- complete, whole, adequate (Colossians 2:10)
- possessing the mind of Christ (1 Corinthians 2:16) and
- loving, joyful, peaceful, patient, kind, etc. (Galatians 5:22-23).

At Restoration

Body
Temple of the Holy Spirit and an instrument of righteousness
Still dying, but yet redeemed
Will be glorified-given a new body

Soul
Mind--has capacity of being renewed
Will--can be empowered by Holy Spirit
Emotions--can be God honoring, and express God's heart

Spirit
Made new and alive to God
Indwelt and sealed with God's Spirit
All of Christ's nature is in me--desires to please God

Our spirit is now indwelt by God's Spirit:

- Our spirit has been sealed with the Holy Spirit (Ephesians 1:13)
- We are now one spirit with Christ (1Corinthians 6:17)
- Our body is the temple of the Holy Spirit (1 Corinthians 3:16 and
- The Holy Spirit desires to live through our soul and body (Galatians 2:20).

Why Are My Actions Inconsistent With My New Identity?

The roadblocks to experiencing our new identity:

Our spirit has been made new. However, our souls and bodies are not new. Because of our new spirit, our souls are now able to receive purity, righteousness and holiness and are being conformed (sanctified) to Truth (Christ) who dwells within us. Our souls are being conformed and our bodies will be made new. Below are some of the "roadblocks" that hinder us from living out of our new identity.

1. An unrenewed mind. Even though our spirits are new, our minds are still programmed with old thought patterns and lies. This is the reason God's word tells us to renew our minds. (Romans 12:2).

2. The flesh. It is the memory of our old way of life when we lived independent of God with the motto, "if it is to be, it's up to me." It is how we got our needs met apart from God. The flesh consists of

Copyright 1998, 2001, 2005, 2007, 2019, 2020 Scope Ministries International, INC.

beliefs, thoughts, feelings, and habits we developed during our life that can play over in our minds like a melody that lingers after the song is over. But this is **not** who we are! (2 Corinthians 5:17; Colossians 2:13-15).

3. Satan. He tempts us by appealing to the memory of the old nature and enticing us to walk in our old ways rather than by the Spirit. His strategy is to deceive and lie to us so we will not believe we have been changed and can live out of our new nature in Christ. (Galatians 2:20).

4. The world system. Media, culture, politics, academia, etc., are part of the world system that Satan uses to deceive us into believing lies as truth. The world tries to conform us into its way of thinking (Romans 12:2) and appeals to our old desires (1 John 2:16). Unfortunately, most of our beliefs about ourselves result from the world system, not God's Word. Our habit has been to rely on our soul and body, not our spirit. For this reason, our soul continually needs to be renewed with truth. (Ephesians 5:18). The truth will set you free. (John 8:31).

> *"But I say walk by the Spirit, and you will not carry out the desire of the flesh. For the flesh sets is desire against the Spirit, and the Spirit against the flesh; for these things are in opposition to one another, so that you may not do the things that you please."* Galatians 5:16-17 NASB

We Can Experience Our New Identity!

We can experience our new identity on a daily, moment-by-moment basis because we have been given "all things that pertain to life and godliness" and we are now partakers of His divine nature all because of the indwelling Christ who lives in us.

> *"To those who have obtained like precious faith with us by the righteousness of our God and Savior Jesus Christ: Grace and peace be multiplied to you in the knowledge of God and of Jesus our Lord. as His divine power has given to us all things that pertain to life and godliness, through the knowledge of Him who call us by glory and virtue, by which have been given to us exceedingly great and precious promise, that through these you may be partakers of the divine nature, having escaped the corruption that is in the world through lust."* 2 Peter 1:1-4 NKJV

We progressively manifest through our soul and body who God has made us in our spirit.

The **GOAL** of experiencing your new identity is to become like Christ (Romans 8:29). This is not accomplished through our own activities and works, but by God who works in us and through us according to His good pleasure (Ephesians 2:13). This is **100% God's part** (1 Thessalonians 5:24).

Copyright 1998, 2001, 2005, 2007, 2019, 2020 Scope Ministries International, INC.

Your New Identity

Faith is receiving the works of God. Faith does not generate the works of God.

The **MEANS** of experiencing the Christ life within has been given to us by God. The Holy Spirit is a person, not just a divine power (John 14:16-17). The Holy Spirit within us enables us to understand and experience who we are in Christ (1 John 16:12-13). This is also **100% God's part**.

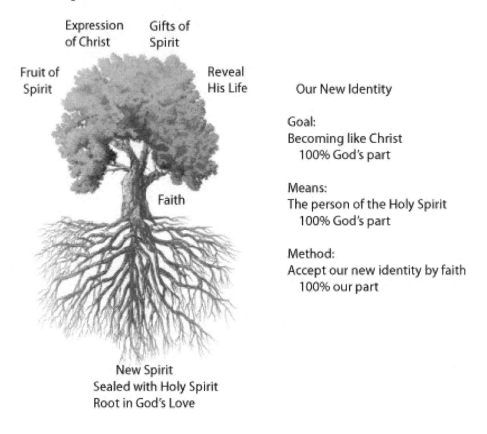

The **METHOD** of experiencing our new identity in Christ is to respond to God **by faith** (Hebrews 11:1, 6; Colossians 2:6; 1 John 5:4-5). We accept by **faith** the power of the cross (that our old sinful nature was crucified with Christ, it died and is no longer our identity) and embrace the reality of our new resurrection life (having been raised up with Christ) (Romans 5:10; 6:5-6). This is **100% our part**. We are to recognize and receive the free gift of salvation and live in the conscious reality of that gift (Colossians 2:6; Ephesians 2:8-10).

Our part is to accept by faith what God says is true about Himself and who He has made us to be in Christ and to walk in the truth of our new identity (1 John 4:17; Romans 8:11,16).

> *"I am crucified with Christ: nevertheless I live; yet not I, but Christ liveth in me: and the life which I now live in the flesh I live by the faith of the Son of God, who loved me, and gave himself for me."* Galatians 2:20 KJV

Faith is releasing that which is already present — Christ's life.

Copyright 1998, 2001, 2005, 2007, 2019, 2020   Scope Ministries International, INC.

Experiencing our new identity in Christ involves choosing to reject the lies we believe about ourselves, replacing them with the truth of who we are in Christ.

The Truest Thing About Us is What God Says!

We learn to act upon the truth regardless of our feelings, experiences, present circumstances, or others' opinions (Philippians 3:12-14).

This is not passivity or inactivity. True faith involves participating in a relationship with Christ, listening to the Holy Spirit, and trusting Him to live through us. Experiencing our new identity in Christ involves living by the truth of the Spirit rather than the melody of the old nature.

Summary

1. We have a three-part nature consisting of our spirit, soul, and body, patterned after God who exists as a Trinity of Father, Son, and Holy Spirit.

2. We were created in the image of God to display the character of God. The Fall affected all three parts of our nature: spirit, soul and body. Most significantly, our spirit died to God.

3. Through our co-crucifixion with Christ, God's image in us is restored. The result of Christ's death, burial, and resurrection was our being given a new spirit and a new identity.

4. Our inability to experience our new identity relates to our unrenewed mind, the flesh, Satan, and the world system.

5. To most fully live out our new identity, we accept it as a fact, by faith, and walk according to the leading of the Holy Spirit who guides and enables us to live externally all that is within us . . . Christ!

The truest thing about me is what God says.

Not what I think or feel and not what others say or think or do.

A Life Transformed, con't.

When I began to learn who I am in Christ, I no longer needed to perform to gain acceptance of God and others. He says that I am complete in Christ, that I am adequate, righteous, holy, that I am a joint heir with Christ, and that I share equally in His inheritance. I am a saint, and I never even taught Sunday School! Wow!

My life is different because my beliefs are different. As a young adult, I was reserved and shy and had a hard time introducing myself to people, individually or in a group. If people didn't introduce themselves to me, I felt as if nobody liked me and that they had rejected me because I wasn't acceptable as Rob. I had to earn their acceptance. Now I know I can go into a group of people and be confident of myself because I am confident about my position in Christ and my attributes in Christ.

When I saw a person who had an asset or strength that I wanted, my standard was to be like that person. Because I was not that person, I never could reach that standard, and I felt unacceptable. Now I don't compare myself with others. For example, I love to listen to the radio commentator Paul Harvey. He's a very eloquent communicator and an excellent storyteller. I would love to be like him, but the truth is that I'm not Paul Harvey. I'm just an ol' country redneck from Oklahoma, but I don't feel unacceptable any more. I understand my strengths, and I no longer have to be like somebody else.

If I'm not in church every time the door is open, I don't feel guilty. My motivation to have a quiet time and memorize Scripture is not to gain approval by God. Now I do these things because He first loved me, and I want to know Him more.

I now know that I don't have to work to be accepted by anybody, including God. John 8:32 says, "You shall know the truth. And the truth will set you free." He has set me free!

Rob - Real Estate Management

The Truth of Your New Identity - Day One

Goal: To understand what Scripture teaches about the nature of a child of God.

Before we can address our problem from God's perspective, we must see ourselves from God's perspective. It is important to realize that the dominant image of man in Scripture is as a whole being. That is, the terms body, soul, and spirit are frequently used interchangeably to mean "life." For example, Romans 12:1 teaches us to present our bodies to God.

> *I urge you therefore, brethren, by the mercies of God, to present your bodies a living and holy sacrifice, acceptable to God, which is your spiritual service of worship.* Romans 12:1 NASB

When we present our bodies to God, we present our whole life.

Although Scripture addresses us as whole beings, it uses the terms body, soul and spirit, also to teach us how we are to function within that whole.

> *Now may the God of peace Himself sanctify you entirely; and may your spirit and soul and body be preserved complete, without blame at the coming of our Lord Jesus Christ.* I Thessalonians 5:23 NAS

1. What do the following passages tell you about the human spirit?

> *Then shall the dust [out of which God made man's body] return to the earth as it was, and the spirit shall return to God Who gave it.* Ecclesiastes 12:7 Amplified

> *God is a Spirit (a spiritual Being) and those who worship Him must worship Him in spirit and in truth (reality).* John 4:24 Amplified

> *The Spirit Himself [thus] testifies together with our own spirit, [assuring us] that we are children of God.* Romans 8:16 Amplified

Remembering that the body is our vehicle of performance or doing, our soul is our thinking, feeling and choosing, and our spirit is our life and identity.

2. List the characteristics of your old identity found in Ephesians 2:1-3; 4:17-22 as they relate to your body, soul, and spirit. Put the characteristics of the old identity under column titled Old Identity on the next page.

3. List the characteristics of your new identity in Christ found in Ezekiel 36:26-27, Romans 6:11, Romans 8:10, 16, Ephesians 4:24, Colossians 3:10-12, Galatians 5:22-23, and as they relate to your body, soul, and spirit. Write the characteristics of your new identity under the column titled New Identity.

Copyright 1998, 2001, 2005, 2007, 2019, 2020 Scope Ministries International, INC.

Old Identity   **New Identity**

4. Based on what you have learned, what kind of nature do Christians have?

5, Write a thank-you note to God expressing gratefulness for His giving you a new spirit (nature).

The Truth of Your New Identity - Day Two

Goal: To begin accepting your new identity.

The following verses reveal that at salvation we were made into new beings. Although this is a reality, the understanding of our new nature becomes ingrained into the very fabric of our identity. Remember that your spirit has been changed, but your soul is in the process of being renewed.

> *A new heart will I give you and a new spirit will I put within you, and I will take away the stony heart out of your flesh and give you a heart of flesh. And I will put My Spirit within you . . .*
> Ezekiel 36:26-27a Amplified
>
> *Therefore, if any man is in Christ, he is a new creature, the old things passed away; behold, new things have come.* 2 Corinthians 5:17 NASB

Read the chart on page 85

1. Select five statements from the first column on page 85 which reflect how you most often view yourself and write them below.

2. Now write out the corresponding truth from the second column and one of the verses given in the third column.

3. Write any thoughts or feelings you have which contradict this truth.

4. How do these negative thoughts affect your daily life?

your behavior?

your emotions?

your relationships?

5. The truest thing about you is what God says! These amazing truths can permeate your thinking and define how you see yourself so that you see life in light of who you are in Christ. Spend a few minutes thanking God for your salvation and for giving you a new spirit and a new identity.

The Truth of Your New Identity - Day Three

Goal: To understand the person and role of the Holy Spirit in our lives.

1. The Holy Spirit is a person, not just a "power." Jesus calls Him, "the Spirit of Truth," "the Comforter," and "the Helper." After each verse below write the role of the Holy Spirit in the Christian's life.

But the Comforter (Counselor, Helper, Intercessor, Advocate, Strengthener, Standby), the Holy Spirit, Whom the Father will send in My Name [in My place, to represent Me and act on My behalf], He will teach you all things. And He will cause you to recall (will remind you of, bring to your remembrance) everything I have told you. John 14:26 Amplified

But when the Comforter (Counselor, Helper, Advocate, Intercessor, Strengthener, Standby) comes, Whom I will send to you from the Father, the Spirit of Truth Who comes (proceeds) from the Father, He [Himself] will testify regarding Me. John 15:26 Amplified

But when He, the Spirit of Truth (the Truth-giving Spirit) comes, He will guide you into all the Truth (the whole, full Truth). For He will not speak His own message [on His own authority]; but He will tell whatever He hears [from the Father; He will give the message that has been given to Him], and He will announce and declare to you the things that are to come [that will happen in the future]. John 16:13 Amplified

Such hope never disappoints or deludes or shames us, for God's love has been poured out in our hearts through the Holy Spirit Who has been given to us. Romans 5:5 Amplified

In the same way the [Holy] Spirit comes to our aid and bears us up in our weakness; for we do not know what prayer to offer nor how to offer it worthily as we ought, but the Spirit Himself goes to meet our supplication and pleads in our behalf with unspeakable yearnings and groanings too deep for utterance. Romans 8:26 Amplified

Now we have not received the spirit [that belongs to] the world, but the [Holy] Spirit Who is from God, [given to us] that we might realize and comprehend and appreciate the gifts [of divine favor and blessing so freely and lavishly] bestowed on us by God. 1 Corinthians 2:12 Amplified

But the fruit of the [Holy] Spirit [the work which His presence within accomplishes] is love, joy (gladness), peace, patience (an even temper, forbearance), kindness, goodness (benevolence), faithfulness, gentleness (meekness, humility), self-control (self-restraint, continence). Against such things there is no law [that can bring a charge]. Galatians 5:22-23 Amplified

2. Review your answers to question 1 and identify the areas for which you have been feeling responsible but which are actually the responsibility of the Holy Spirit.

3. The Holy Spirit is responsible for conforming us to Christ. Express your gratitude to God for the Holy Spirit's presence and ministry in your life. Admit to God the areas in which you have not acknowledged the Holy Spirit or depended on Him for your spiritual development.

The Truth of Your New Identity - Day Four

Goal: To recognize that your part in experiencing your new identity is to live by faith

The method of experiencing your new identity is to live by faith. Faith is taking God at His Word. Faith is our response to the revelation of Who God is and what He has done for us through Christ. Faith is a gift of God (Ephesians 2:8-9) which can increase over time, much like a muscle that grows stronger with use.

1. What does the following verse tell you regarding how we are saved?

> *Because if you acknowledge and confess with your lips that Jesus is Lord and in your heart believe (adhere to, trust in, and rely on the truth) that God raised Him from the dead, you will be saved. For with the heart a person believes (adheres to, trusts in, and relies on Christ) and so is justified (declared righteous, acceptable to God), and with the mouth He confesses (declares openly and speaks out freely his faith) and confirms [his] salvation.* Romans 10:9-10 Amplified

2. What does the following verse say regarding faith?

> *So faith comes from hearing, and hearing by the Word of Christ.* Romans 10:17, NASB

3. What does Colossians 2:6 say about how we are to walk (live moment by moment)?

> *As you therefore have received Christ Jesus the Lord, so walk in Him.* Colossians 2:6 NAS

4. According to Galatians 2:20, how are you to live?

> *I have been crucified with Christ [in Him I have shared His crucifixion]; it is no longer I who live, but Christ (the Messiah) lives in me; and the life I now live in the body I live by faith in (by adherence to and reliance on and complete trust in) the Son of God, Who loved me and gave Himself up for me.* Galatians 2:20 Amplified

5. Faith is not a feeling, nor is it intellectual knowledge. Who is to be the object of our faith, according to Hebrews 12:1-2?

> *Therefore, since we have so great a cloud of witnesses surrounding us, let us also lay aside every encumbrance, and the sin which so easily entangles us, and let us run with endurance the race that is set before us, fixing our eyes on Jesus, the author and perfecter of faith, who for the joy set before Him endured the cross, despising the shame, and has sat down at the right hand of the throne of God.* Hebrews 12:1-2 NASB

We are not to put faith in our faith. Biblical faith is trust and reliance on the person and character of God. As you confess your new identity with your mouth and believe in your heart what God has said, the Holy Spirit will make it real in your experience (in God's time, not yours).

6. Spend a few minutes thanking God for your new identity (be specific), and express your trust in Him to make it your experience through the power of the Holy Spirit.

The Truth of Your New Identity - Day Five

Goal: To understand how to experience your new identity, practically, in your daily life.

Experiencing your new identity is more than just a matter of replacing negative thoughts with more positive ones. It is the result of relating to God and believing what He says about who you are in Christ. Daily you choose to put off the old identity and put on your new identity.

1. Read the following passage several times.

> *This I say therefore, and affirm together with the Lord, that you walk no longer just as the Gentiles also walk, in the futility of their mind, being darkened in their understanding, excluded from the life of God, because of the ignorance that is in them, because of the hardness of their heart; and they, having become callous, have given themselves over to sensuality, for the practice of every kind of impurity with greediness. But you did not learn Christ in this way, if indeed you have heard Him and have been taught in Him, just as truth is in Jesus, that, in reference to your former manner of life, you lay aside the old self (identity), which is being corrupted in accordance with the lusts of deceit, and that you be renewed in the spirit of your mind, and put on the new self, which in the likeness of God has been created in righteousness and holiness of the truth.* Ephesians 4:17-24 NAS

2. Ask the Holy Spirit to bring to your mind one area in your life where you are not presently experiencing your new identity in Christ.

3. Ask the Holy Spirit to show you the lies you are believing in this area of your life and the thoughts that need to be replaced with God's Truth. Write the lie that is to be put off and the truth that is to be put on.

4. For each lie you listed, write the truth about your new identity on a 3 x 5 card or post-it note, along with a corresponding verse of Scripture (refer to Day Two). Now place these in prominent places (such as the bathroom mirror, refrigerator, dash of car, etc.) so you will be reminded of the truth throughout the day. When reminded of the truth, thank God (out loud if possible) for what is really true about you "in Christ." Continue this daily for the next three weeks.

The Truth About Your New Idenitiy Lesson Three
Summary

Name

Date

Answer the following questions and turn in page to small group leader.

1. According to what you have learned about the nature of man, what changed in you at salvation?

2. How does understanding that you have a new nature give you confidence concerning your salvation and spiritual growth?

3. What wrong beliefs about yourself do you need to put off?

4. How would believing your new identity and relying on the Holy Spirit in your daily life affect the way you respond to your present problems?

5. What questions do you have concerning the nature of man and your new identity?

6. Mark the graph to indicate how much of this week's assignment you completed.

None ——————————————— 50% ——————————————— 100%

What I Feel or Think About Myself	What Is True About Me According to the Scripture	Scripture References
I am unworthy/unacceptable.	I am accepted/worthy.	Ps 139; Rom 15:7
I am alone.	I am never alone.	Heb 13:5b; Rom 8:38-39
I feel like a failure/inadequate.	I am adequate.	2 Cor 3:5-6; Phil 4:13
I have no confidence.	I have all the boldness/confidence I need.	Prov 3:26, 14:26, 28:1; Eph 3:12; Heb 10:19;
I feel responsible for my life.	God is responsible/faithful to me.	Ps 138:8; Phil 1:6, 2:13; 2 Thes 3:3
I am confused/think I am going crazy.	I have the mind of Christ.	1 Cor 2:16; 2 Tim 1:7; Eph 1:17
I am depressed/hopeless.	I have all the hope I need.	Ps 27:13, 31:24; Rom 15:13, 5:5; Heb 6:19
I am not good enough/imperfect.	I am perfect in Christ.	Heb 10:14; Col 2:10; Eph 2:10
There is nothing special about me.	I have been chosen/set apart by God.	Ps 139; 1 Cor 1:30, 6:11; 2 Thes 2:13
I don't have enough.	I have no lack.	Psalm 23:1; Phil 4:19
I am a fearful/anxious person.	I am free from fear.	Ps 34:4; 2 Tim 1:7; 1 Pet 5:7; 1 Jn 4:18
I lack faith.	I have all the faith I need.	Rom 10:17; 12:3, Heb 12:2
I am a weak person.	I am strong in Christ.	Dan 11:32; Is 58:11; Phil 4:13
I am defeated.	I am victorious.	Rom 8:37; 2 Cor 2:14; Jn 5:4
I am not very smart.	I have God's wisdom.	Prov 2:6-7; 1 Cor 1:30; Eph 1:17
I am in bondage.	I am free in Christ.	Ps 32:7; 2 Cor 3:17; Jn 8:36
I am miserable.	I have God's comfort.	Jn 16:7; 2 Cor 1:3-4
I have no one to take care of me.	I am protected/safe.	Ps 32:7; Ps 91
I am unloved.	I am very loved.	Jn 15:9; Rom 8:38-39; Eph 2:4, 5:1-2
I am unwanted/I don't belong to anyone.	I have been adopted by God. I am His child.	Rom 8:16-17; Gal 4:5; Eph 1:5; 1 Jn 3:1-2
I feel guilty.	I am totally forgiven/redeemed.	Ps 103:12; Eph 1:7; Col 1:14, 20; Col 2:13-14; Heb 10:10
I am a sinner.	I have been declared holy, righteous and justified. I am a saint.	Rom 3:24; 1 Cor 1:30, 6:11; 2 Cor 5:21
I have no strength.	I have God's power. I am indwelt with the Holy Spirit.	Acts 1:8; Rom 8:9-11; Eph 1:19, 3:16
I can't reach God.	I have direct access to God as a believer-priest.	Eph 2:6; Heb 10:19-20; 1 Pet 2:5,9
I feel condemned.	I am uncondemned/blameless.	Jn 3:18; Rom 8:1; Col 1:22
There is no direction/plan.	God does direct my life/He has a plan for me.	Ps 37:23, 138:8; Jer 29:11; Eph 2:10
I feel like nothing will ever change.	I've been given a brand new life.	2 Cor 5:17; Eph 4:22-24
I am afraid of Satan.	I have authority over Satan.	Col 1:13; 1 Jn 4:4; Rev 12:11
Sin overpowers me.	I am dead to sin.	Rom 6:6,11, 17-18

The Truth About God

If you had known Me, you would have known My Father also; from now on you know Him, and have seen Him . . . He who has seen Me has seen the Father . . .

John 14:7, 9b NASB

Lesson Four

A Life Transformed

Three years ago, I didn't want to live. I was controlled by fear and shame. I couldn't look anyone in the eye.

And I was a Christian. I spoke the "right" words from my mouth about who God is. I talked as if I knew Him and I had a relationship with Him, but, deep inside, the thought of God as my loving Father physically made me sick. I believed that God lurked in the shadows, ready to use me and punish me.

Obviously my view of God was twisted. With both of my parents involved in the occult, I learned from infancy to see God as my enemy. Instead of bonding with my parents, I clung to darkness and the hidden. The rituals of satanic worship consumed me even before I could talk. I thought the sexual abuse was love. Shame was ever-present in my life.

In 1989, I was weary of life, and I gave my life to Jesus because I didn't want to go to hell. But I didn't want to trust Him to love me. Instead I relied on prescription drugs while I filled my head with knowledge about God, but I still didn't know Him. I was trapped in a darkness of lies and deception that my human reason couldn't reveal. I thought that I was such a bad person that I was driven to punish myself through self-mutilation and other destructive behaviors because I felt I deserved to be punished.

I was withdrawn and depressed. I couldn't live this life anymore. I planned a quiet death, but God intervened. I began a journey that I thought was about me and was going nowhere, but this journey was really about God and journeying from my darkness towards His light.

to be continued...

The Truth About God
Lesson Four

In the last lesson we have looked at our beliefs (The Truth about Lies). We have seen how faulty beliefs have adversely affected us. In this lesson we will discover how our beliefs about God affect us. We will see how our beliefs about God develop early in our lives through our relationships, especially parental relationships.

A. W. Tozer, an American-born pastor from the first half of the twentieth century, wrote in his well known book, <u>The Knowledge of the Holy</u>, "What comes to our minds when we think about God is the most important thing about us."

Our Perception of God Affects the Quality of Our Lives

How we see God affects every area of our lives.

Our inaccurate beliefs about God hinder us from enjoying an intimate relationship with Him. Our distorted perception of God affects:

- The purpose and meaning we give to life Philippians 3:8

- How we interpret the circumstances and events in our lives 2 Corinthians 4:16-18

- The degree to which we will come to love and trust God Psalm 22:4-5; 1 Thessalonians 5:24

- How we see ourselves Numbers 13:33

- How we relate to others 1 John 4:8

   Grace and peace be multiplied to you in the knowledge of God and of Jesus our Lord; seeing that His divine power has granted to us everything pertaining to life and godliness, through the true knowledge of Him who called us by His own glory and excellence. For by these He has granted to us His precious and magnificent promises, in order that by them you might become partakers of the divine nature, having escaped the corruption that is in the world by lust.   2 Peter 1:2-4 NASB

Our relationship with God, self, and others was changed at the Fall.

As we learned in lesson one, in the Garden God warned Adam about the consequences of eating the fruit from one tree. Satan deceived Eve by challenging God's word and planting doubt in her mind concerning God's character. Doubting God's character and His intentions toward

them, Eve and Adam declared their independence from God by eating from the Tree of Knowledge of Good and Evil. Since that time, man has determined for himself what is true or false, good or evil, right or wrong, based on his senses, reason, and emotions. Because man's spirit died to the things of God, he could no longer know and communicate with God as his Father.

The result of Adam and Eve's decision for independence was spiritual death. All life, spiritual and physical, comes from God. Any attempt to produce life apart from God is deficient and will fail. It will, at best, be a sad imitation of God's original design. By his choice, Adam changed the spiritual trajectory of all mankind. Separated from the true Source of Life, Adam must look for life, meaning, and fulfillment from others, rather than God. He must rely upon his own resources; mind, will and emotions to meet the needs that God once met for him.

Our deepest needs are:
- Love
- Acceptance
- Belonging
- Security
- Approval
- Significance
- Competence and adequacy.

Since we are all descendants of Adam, we also are spiritual orphans, without an ability to know and relate to God. One of our strategies for making life work is to minimize our weaknesses and capitalize on our strengths. For example:

- The exceptionally athletic guy becomes the captain of the football team and enjoys the acceptance and accolades of winning.

- The beautiful young woman relies upon her good looks for affirmation and value.

- The person that is not handsome or beautiful might rely upon humor or intelligence to be accepted and impress others.

Christ has restored us to a permanent father-child relationship with God.

As people who have trusted in Christ, we are now God's children (1 John 3:1-3). We are no longer sinful children of Adam, but righteous children of God. We have a new human spirit, the Holy Spirit indwelling us, and a permanent father-child relationship with God the Father.

Even though our relationship with God has changed, the experience of being a spiritual orphan has affected our belief system about our Heavenly Father. Much of our view of God is incorrect and distorted because it was developed while we were orphans.

On the next two pages you will find a chart listing examples of possible faulty perceptions of God based on key figures from our childhood.

Experiences with our parents and key relationships have influenced our perception of our Heavenly Father.

AUTHORITY FIGURE	LIES WE BELIEVE ABOUT		HOW MY BELIEFS AFFECT MY RELATIONSHIPS
	GOD	SELF	
Authoritarian			
Lies	God is more concerned with compliance than relationship.	I am insignificant.	I seek other's approval. I try to show that I am valuable.
	He insists on His way.	I am invisible.	I defer to others
Truth	He desires relationship and intimacy.	I am valuable and cherished.	I can love others without needing their approval.
	He is interested in my opinions, desires, and goals.		
Verses	John 17:20-23; Eph 1:3-13; Luke 24:13-35; John 3:16; Eph 2:10; 2 Cor 5:17; Rom 8:17; 15:7; 12:9-18; 1 Pet 5:7; Phil 3:20		
Abusive			
Lies	God is cruel. He is punishing. He is against me.	I am powerless. I need to protect myself at any cost.	Everyone has ulterior motives.
	God is not trustworthy.	My value is determined only by how I am useful to others.	It is difficult to trust others and establish relationships.
Truth	God is for me. He will not reject me.	I am valuable, acceptable, and safe.	I am willing to be vulnerable in relationships.
	He is a loving Father.	My identity is secure	I am learning to trust others.
	He does not punish.		
Verses	Rom 5:8; 8:15, 31-39; 15:7; 2 Cor 2:1-5; Matt 10:30-31; Psalm 91; John 15:9; 16:27; 17:23b		
Absent/Distant			
Lies	God is not there.	I am abandoned and neglected.	I look for security and belonging from others.
		I have to figure out life on my own.	I am attracted to strong people.
Truth	The Holy Spirit lives within me.	I am never alone nor forsaken.	I am not looking for security and a sense of belonging from others.
	He is joyfully involved in my life. Zeph 3:17	I have worth.	
	He likes me.	I am lovable and enjoyed.	
Verses	Heb 13:5; 1 Cor 3:16; 2 Cor 5:21; 1 John 4:16; John 1:12; 15:9; 16:27; 17:23b; 21:15-19		

AUTHORITY FIGURE	LIES WE BELIEVE ABOUT		HOW MY BELIEFS AFFECT MY RELATIONSHIPS
	GOD	SELF	
Passive			
Lies	God is uninvolved in my life and does not care enough to share in my joy and pain.	I am not valuable to God. I am a nuisance.	I am not valuable to others. I am continually seeking reassurance and affirmation from others.
		Because God is not involved, I am responsible for my life and other people's lives.	I'm scared to ask for what I need, so I manipulate.
			I need to control others to make myself feel secure.
Truth	He is in union with us. We are one with Him.	I am acceptable.	I can trust God to meet my needs. I can trust God in other people's lives.
	No one knows me and loves me more than Him.	I am embraced and loved.	Since God is for me I don't need to control or manipulate.
Verses	1 Cor 6:17; John 17:22-24; 15:15; 2 Cor 11:2; 12:9-10; Eph 1:7-10; 3:20; Rom 5:1; 8:17; Psalm 56:9; 23:1; Jer 31:3		

AUTHORITY FIGURE	LIES WE BELIEVE ABOUT		HOW MY BELIEFS AFFECT MY RELATIONSHIPS
Critical			
Lies	God judges every failure.	I am a failure. I deserve punishment.	I am looking to others for approval and acceptance. Their approval is tied to my performance.
	He is impossible to please. I can never reach His standards.		I hide my failures.
			I am judgmental and critical toward others.
Truth	He is for me	I am not a failure	Because I am acceptable to God, I don't need to compare myself to others.
	He is encouraging	I am the recipient of God's grace.	
	He doesn't condemn		
Verses	Psalm 56:9; Rom 8:31; 5:2; 8:10; 15:7; 2 Cor 2:14; 5:21; Eph 2:7; 2:8-9; 1:4; Col 1:22; Phil 4:13; 2 Cor 3:3-6		

Our initial concepts of God develop early in life from our relationships and experiences with authority figures, such as father, mother, grandparents, etc.. Generally, the most significant relationship which influences our perception of God is our relationship with our earthly father. Often, the more negative or painful the relationship is or was, the more distorted our view of God is.

Our view of God as Father is often derived from:

- Our personal experiences with those key figures in our lives; most often our parents, grandparents, or significant relationships

- Unmet needs from our relationship with these key relationships

- The world's information about what they are supposed to look like

- False or incomplete information about God

If you then being evil, know how to give good gifts to your children, how much more shall your heavenly Father give the Holy Spirit to those who ask Him?   Luke 11:13 NASB

As spiritual orphans we envisioned in our minds an image of God as Father based upon our experiences with our earthly father. Some of us had very good and very involved fathers, so the effects of emotional and physical absence are not as drastic in our lives as in the lives of others. However, even if we have outstanding earthly fathers, they are still imperfect and will never give us a complete and accurate view of who God is as Father. We all still need to know God as the perfect Father.

We Need to Know Our Heavenly Father for Who He Really Is

Tozer gives us a wonderful perspective of God, "An infinite, God can give all of Himself to each of His children. He does not distribute Himself that each may have a part, but to each one He gives all of Himself as fully as if there were no others"

We are worshipping beings and become like the one we worship.

Psalm 115:1-8 reveals that we become like that which we worship. In fact, the essence of Eternal Life is to know God the Father intimately

through Jesus Christ (John 17:3). The more we know Him, the more we are like Christ. The more we are like Him, the more we desire to know Him and be in relationship with Him.

However, without a proper view of God, we will create a false or incomplete view of God and worship this image (Romans 1:18-32). This is Satan's objective! Although, he can't take away our salvation, he desires to limit our relationship with God by distorting our view of God. He knows that if we do not worship God as He really is, we will not become like Him.

Our real beliefs about God are revealed by our lives. How we respond to God during difficult times and the way we treat and relate to others reveal a lot about how we see God.

> *In this you greatly rejoice, even though now for a little while, if necessary, you have been distressed by various trials, that the proof of your faith, being more precious than gold which is perishable, even though tested by fire, may be found to result in praise and glory and honor at the revelation of Jesus Christ; and though you have not seen Him, you love Him, and though you do not see Him now, but believe in Him, you greatly rejoice with joy inexpressible and full of glory.*
> 1 Peter 1:6-8 NASB

The more we know God as He really is, the more we love Him. The more we love Him, the more we become like Him. The more we become like Him, the more we desire to know Him.

> *Beloved, let us love one another, for love is from God; and everyone who loves is born of God and knows God. The one who does not love does not know God, for God is love.* 1 John 4:7-8 NASB

Jesus reveals our Heavenly Father

Jesus is the visible expression of our Heavenly Father. Through Jesus we can come to know the character and heart of our heavenly Father.

> *And the Word became flesh, and dwelt among us, and we beheld His glory, glory as of the only begotten from the Father, full of grace and truth.*
> John 1:14 NASB

> *If you had known Me, you would have known My Father also; from now on you know Him, and have seen Him . . . He who has seen Me has seen the Father.* John 14:7,9b NASB

We may know a lot about God but still not relate to Him as Jesus revealed Him or as Scripture teaches about Him. If we know God as He truly is, we can regain a true father-child relationship with Him, and then we can image or express His likeness.

God's Word reveals our Father

We approach Scripture for what it says, rather than reading our experience into it. If we read Scripture without exploring what wrong perceptions we have about God, we may project passivity, disinterest, or meanness that we have assumed to be true of God. We may have attributed to God feelings we have about our own earthly authority figures.

When we read God's Word, we depend on the Holy Spirit to reveal God's character and the Living Word.

Some important truths that God reveals to us in Scripture:

- It is God's desire for you to come to know him as your Heavenly Father. John 17:20-22

- God is our Abba or Daddy. See Romans 8:15-17. Paul uses a term here that was used by small children, much as we might say *dada*. We can trust God like a small child unreservedly trusts his daddy. However, unlike some of our dads, God never changes or fails in His nurturing for us.

- God loves us unconditionally. Romans 5:8, 1 John 4:19. God's love is not based upon how well we perform for him. His love predates any of our good deeds. His love is due to His character, not ours.

- God desires nothing but the best for us. Jeremiah 29:11. Romans 8:28-29. God does not want you to live in bondage to sin, compulsions, or obsessions of any sort. He is in the process of conforming you into the image of His Son.

- God knows you intimately and delights in you Psalms 18:19; Zephaniah 3:17. Delighting is taking active pleasure in a person. When we feel disgusted with ourselves or when we fail, God still delights in us. This is very difficult to believe, because all we can see is our faults.

- Because God is love 1 John 4:8,16, we can view the "love passage" in 1 Corinthians 13 as a description of God. Read 1 Corinthians 13, replacing the word "love" (or charity) with "God"

- God is not condemning of you. Romans 5:8, 8:1. He does not condemn you for areas in which you continue to fail. He is using these very struggles to show you He is sufficient to meet your needs in every area of your life. Jesus Christ will be All THAT HE IS TO ALL THAT YOU NEED. He is ENOUGH. Philippians 4:19

- God does not view you the same way as others do. 1 Samuel 16:7. He has cleansed, forgiven, justified, and made you acceptable and compatible with Him, equipped you with a new heart, a new spirit, replaced the old man, gave you a pliable heart, and sent the Holy Spirit to live inside of you. This has all been completed and can never be undone. His life has been placed inside of you, giving you life as long as He lives! Romans 5:1; Romans 6-8; Ezekiel 36:26-27; 2 Corinthians 5:17; Colossians 2:13; 3:13

We Need to See Ourselves as God's Adopted Children

We are God's spirit-born sons and daughters

Being a child of God makes us either a prince or a princess. Therefore we are all beings of worth and value. Christ's presence within us gives us worth. We are placed in Christ and Christ is placed in us, making us one with Him. Some other exciting truths that result from our new standing as children of God are that:

- We are totally forgiven by our Father—Ephesians 1:3-7; 2:4-5
- We have His Holy Spirit to teach and remind us—John 14:26
- Our Father loves us the same as He loves Jesus—John 16:27, 17:23
- Our Father has made us acceptable and delights in us—Zephaniah 3:17; Romans 15:7; Colossians 1:22
- Our Father is committed to transforming us—Romans 8:29, Philippians 1:6

We need to acknowledge our adoption as God's beloved children and relate to Him as our Heavenly ABBA.

We allow God to renew our minds about God

We need to think in day-to-day situations according to our new beliefs about God as our Father. We need to view our circumstances in light of our loving Heavenly Father's care, putting our trust in Him and His ultimate purposes for us (Romans 8:28; Jeremiah 29:11).

We choose to act and react according to Who God is

Depending on the Holy Spirit, we learn to act on our new thoughts and beliefs. This is how we live in a faith relationship with God.

NOTE:

It is important that we not blame our authority figures for our wrong view of God. Our real enemy is Satan, the father of lies. The good news is that our Heavenly Father has made possible knowing Him as He really is through Jesus Christ. However, there are not three easy steps to a good God concept. Knowing God is a life-long process which involves more than having the right knowledge about God. It is experientially knowing and trusting His true character in the midst of life's circumstances. Remember, this can only be accomplished through the empowering presence of the Holy Spirit in our lives.

Summary:

1. How we view God affects the quality of our lives.

2. Our experiences within our key relationships have influenced our concept of God.

3. We can know our Heavenly Father as He really is through Jesus and through renewing our minds with Scripture.

4. As our minds are renewed we relate to Him as His dearly loved children.

A Life Transformed, con't.

God began to expose the darkness in my soul and my mind and my body, and He began to reveal Himself to me as He truly is. I met the real Jesus in whom there is no darkness at all, and He gave me a safe way to think about Him - as a bright light.

Gradually, God's truth began to push out the deeply rooted lies about who He is and who I am. I had believed that He was punishing me by withholding good things from me. Now I know that He loves me, that He knows best what I need, and He gives it to me. I thought that He had abandoned me while I was being abused and that He would abandon me again. Now I know that He was with me when I was abused and that He will give me justice. I am sure that He will never leave me.

He restored my childhood to me - in a sense - by using children in my life to show me how to relate to Him. I began to talk to Him, sharing more and more with Him. I began to trust Him in little things, and I became willing to receive from Him in little ways. I began to express my emotions to Him no matter how raw or immature they seemed. I learned that even when I was angry with Him, I was still safe just being with Him and letting Him love me.

Many beliefs I had about me changed too. I no longer believe that I am an orphan, repulsive to God, worthless, dirty, marked, and defiled. I now believe that I am chosen, accepted, loved, cleansed, forgiven, and holy.

As I changed on the inside, I changed on the outside, but I didn't even see the changes at first. I learned to listen to God through journaling and music. I began to experience freedom in worship and praise. I broke the code of silence and was able to shout to the Lord with joy. I would catch myself laughing. I could call God Father.

I no longer believed that I had to make myself clean and worthy so that I could be good enough to receive His love. My desire to receive His love was stronger than my desire to hurt or punish myself. I was finally free to receive His love.

As I began to receive His love, I no longer had to seek it from other people. I'm not afraid that I'll lose the relationship if I don't do everything right. I don't have to take responsibility for everything. I don't have to control and manipulate others and circumstances. Instead of my neediness being the driving force in relationships, now love is.

My journey continues. God is my Father, and I know that He really loves me. To paraphrase 1 Peter 2:9, God has called me out of my darkness, and now I live in His wonderful light.

Cyndee - Assistant Bookkeeper

The Truth About God - Day One

Goal: To recognize how your earthly father (or other authority figure) has influenced your emotional perception of God as your Heavenly Father.

1. Write a description of who your earthly father is to you.

2. Write who God the Father is to you (based on your emotional—not intellectual understanding of God).

3. Do you see any correlation between the way you view your earthly father and the way you view God as your Father? If so, in what ways?

4. Until we recognize the lies we're believing about God, we will probably not trust Him enough to turn to Him in a time of need or develop a close, intimate relationship with Him. Below are some common wrong perceptions we have about God.

   Evaluate your emotional perception of God (not what you know to be true) by circling the number that best describes your thoughts and feelings.

   0 = never 1 = seldom 2 = sometimes 3 = often 4 = usually 5 = always

Generally, in my relationship with God I feel:

Nothing (I don't feel His presence at all)	0	1	2	3	4	5
Abandoned (I have to do things myself)	0	1	2	3	4	5
Alone (I'm all by myself for solutions and strength)	0	1	2	3	4	5
Unsure (of what He thinks of me or where I stand with Him)	0	1	2	3	4	5
Uneasy (I don't know what to expect)	0	1	2	3	4	5

Generally I feel God is:

Inconsiderate (He doesn't take into account my feelings and forces me to do things I don't want to do or doesn't let me do things I want to do)	0	1	2	3	4	5
Hard to please (No matter what I do, it isn't good enough; or, I can't know what is expected from me;	0	1	2	3	4	5
Conditionally loving (His love for me is based on my obedience)	0	1	2	3	4	5
Unloving (He sees my situation and allows me to suffer)	0	1	2	3	4	5

Angry/Judgmental (He is quick to punish me when I don't measure up; turns His back on me when I fail)	0	1	2	3	4	5
Impatient (He wants things done now!)	0	1	2	3	4	5
Critical (Most of what He thinks or says to me is negative)	0	1	2	3	4	5
Punishing (He's mad and withdraws or punishes me when I sin)	0	1	2	3	4	5
Hard to hear (I don't hear from Him, or I vaguely hear from Him)	0	1	2	3	4	5
Non-communicative (He doesn't talk to me much or at all)	0	1	2	3	4	5
Hard to understand (can't quite figure Him out—complicated)	0	1	2	3	4	5
Not helping me (I'm left to do it in my own strength)	0	1	2	3	4	5
Irresponsible (He's allowing all sorts of bad things to happen)	0	1	2	3	4	5
Slow (He takes His time changing me or getting things done)	0	1	2	3	4	5
Uncaring (He really doesn't care)	0	1	2	3	4	5
Tolerating my presence (He doesn't prefer me)	0	1	2	3	4	5

5. Now list the characteristics of God for which you circled 3 or higher on question 4.

6. What does the following verse tell you about your Heavenly Father?

> *No man has ever seen God at any time; the only unique Son, or the only-begotten God, Who is in the bosom [in the intimate presence] of the Father, He has declared Him [He has revealed Him and brought Him out where He can be seen; He has interpreted Him and He has made Him known].* John 1:18 Amplified

7. What does Jesus claim in the following verses?

> *Jesus said to him, "I am the Way and the Truth and the Life; no one comes to the Father except by (through) Me. If you had known Me [had learned to recognize Me], you would also have known My Father. From now on, you know Him and have seen Him." Philip said to Him, "Lord, show us the Father [cause us to see the Father—that is all we ask]; then we shall be satisfied." Jesus replied, "Have I been with all of you for so long a time, and do you not recognize and know Me yet, Philip? Anyone who has seen Me has seen the Father. How can you say then, Show us the Father? Do you not believe that I am in the Father, and that the Father is in Me?"* John 14:6-10a Amplified

8. According to these verses, how can we know what our Heavenly Father is like?

The Truth About God - Day Two

Goal: To recognize and strengthen the areas where your concept of your Heavenly Father is weak or distorted.

1. Relational Evaluation: This exercise allows you to evaluate your relationship with God as your Heavenly Father. Because it is subjective, there are no wrong answers. On a scale of 1-10, rate how real this characteristic is to you in your relationship with your Heavenly Father. Remember you are evaluating how much you experience this characteristic of God.

Do you see your Heavenly Father as One who is:

Characteristic	Never									Always
__ Loving	1	2	3	4	5	6	7	8	9	10
__ Caring	1	2	3	4	5	6	7	8	9	10
__ Forgiving	1	2	3	4	5	6	7	8	9	10
__ Compassionate	1	2	3	4	5	6	7	8	9	10
__ Giving	1	2	3	4	5	6	7	8	9	10
__ Understanding	1	2	3	4	5	6	7	8	9	10
__ Accepting	1	2	3	4	5	6	7	8	9	10
__ Satisfies	1	2	3	4	5	6	7	8	9	10
__ Persistently pursuing	1	2	3	4	5	6	7	8	9	10
__ Reasonable	1	2	3	4	5	6	7	8	9	10

2. Psalm 103 contains many characteristics of our Father-Savior. With each characteristic, provide the corresponding verse. Next, rate yourself as to how real this characteristic is to you in your relationship with God.

Characteristic - Verse	Never									Always
__ Pardons _____	1	2	3	4	5	6	7	8	9	10
__ Heals _____	1	2	3	4	5	6	7	8	9	10
__ Redeems _____	1	2	3	4	5	6	7	8	9	10
__ Lovingkindness _____	1	2	3	4	5	6	7	8	9	10
__ Compassion _____	1	2	3	4	5	6	7	8	9	10
__ Satisfies _____	1	2	3	4	5	6	7	8	9	10
__ Renews _____	1	2	3	4	5	6	7	8	9	10
__ Righteous _____	1	2	3	4	5	6	7	8	9	10
__ Gracious _____	1	2	3	4	5	6	7	8	9	10
__ Sovereign _____	1	2	3	4	5	6	7	8	9	10

A rating of 1 to 6 probably indicates a wrong concept of God as Father-Savior. From this list and the list in question 5, Day One, identify the characteristics you need to experience more fully in your relationship with God and check them on the list below.

Loving —John 3:16; 1 Corinthians 13:4-8; 1 John 4:10
- _____ My Father-Savior loves me for who I am.
- _____ His love for me is unconditional and unceasing.

Caring — Matthew 6:26; 10:29-31; 1 Peter 5:7
- _____My Father-Savior cares for me always.
- _____His major concern is my well-being.

Forgiving — Psalm 103:12; Colossians 1:14; Hebrews 10:17
- _____My Father-Savior has forgiven me unconditionally.
- _____His forgiveness of my sins includes forgetfulness.

Compassionate — Exodus 33:19; Deuteronomy 4:31; Psalm 103:4-5
- _____My Father-Savior is full of compassion toward me.
- _____His compassion affirms me and supports me.

Giving — Psalm 37:4; Romans 8:32; James 1:17
- _____My Father-Savior gives me the desires of my heart.
- _____His giving nature withholds no good thing from me.

Understanding — Job 12:13; Psalm 139:1-2; Isaiah 40:28
- _____My Father-Savior understands my thoughts and my actions.
- _____His understanding of me gives me strength and comfort.

Accepting — Psalm 139:1-6; Romans 15:7
- _____My Father-Savior accepts me totally and unconditionally.
- _____His acceptance of me is based on who I am and not on what I do.

Satisfies — Psalm 107:9; Matthew 6:33; John 14:14; Ephesians 3:19
- _____My Father-Savior fulfills my every need.
- _____His grace provides a canopy of satisfaction for me.

Persistently pursuing — Luke 19:10; 1 Timothy 1:15; 2:4; Titus 2:11
- _____My Father-Savior is the Hound of Heaven.
- _____He moved Heaven and earth to bring me to Him.

Reasonable — Proverbs 3:5-6; Isaiah 1:18; Ephesians 3:12
- _____My Father-Savior is completely approachable.
- _____His attitude toward me is one of favor and good will.

Pardons — Psalm 103:3; Isaiah 43:25; 55:7
- _____My Father-Savior offers me full and free pardon.
- _____He does not take into account the wrongs I have done to Him.

Heals — II Chronicles 7:14; Psalm 147:3; Isaiah 53:5
- _____My Father-Savior is a God Who heals.
- _____His concern for my health and well-being is overwhelming.

Redeems — Job 19:25; Psalm 19:14; Isaiah 63:16
- _____My Father-Savior has redeemed me from all my sin.
- _____His redemption of me is for all eternity.

Lovingkindness — Psalm 86:15; 117:2
- _____My Father-Savior expresses His lovingkindness to me always.
- _____His lovingkindness to me sustains me through everything.

Renews — Isaiah 40:31; II Corinthians 4:16; Titus 3:5
- _____My Father-Savior renews me day by day.
- _____He imparts His strength and power to me.

Righteous — Jeremiah 9:23-24; Psalm 11:7; 1 Corinthians 1:30
- _____My Father-Savior is righteous in all that He does with me.
- _____He imputes righteousness to me, making me righteous.

Gracious — Nehemiah 9:31; Psalm 86:1,15; Ephesians 1:7-8
- _____My Father-Savior is always gracious to me.
- _____He lavishes His graciousness on me as His child.

Sovereign — Psalm 24:8; Psalm 103:19; Revelation 1:8
- _____My Father-Savior is sovereign over all.
- _____He is King of kings and Lord of lords, and I am His child.

Now that you know the characteristics which need to be strengthened in your understanding of God, select one verse for each of those characteristics. Begin renewing your mind about Who your Father is by meditating each day on these verses. Spend some time now writing what your wrong thoughts have been and then write the right thoughts. Spend time talking to God and making a conscious choice to put off the wrong thoughts.

Wrong Thoughts about God Put Off	Right Thoughts about God Put On
Example: 　I don't see how God could possibly love me.	Example: My Father's love is unconditional and unchanging. It is not based on who I am, but Who He is.

The Truth About God - Day Three

Goal: To know the character and heart of God the Father through His Son, Jesus Christ.

1. Describe how you view Jesus as a person.

2. What do the following verses tell you about Jesus?

   I and the Father are One. John 10:30 Amplified

   [Now] He is the exact likeness of the unseen God [the visible representation of the invisible]; He is the Firstborn of all creation. Colossians 1:15 Amplified

   For in Him the whole fullness of Deity (the Godhead) continues to dwell in bodily form [giving complete expression of the divine nature]. Colossians 2:9 Amplified

3. Compare your view of Jesus with your view of God the Father from Day One. What are the similarities and / or differences?

Often our view of Jesus is very different from our view of God. Why? Because we have developed our view of Jesus from the stories about Him in the Gospels. We also have based our view of God on our past experiences with authoritive figures (father, mother, etc.).

4. Read the following Scriptures and write how each verse describes Jesus.

Luke 19:10 _____

Matthew 9:10-13 _____

Matthew 9:36 _____

Matthew 11:28-30 _____

Matthew 23:37 _____

John 8:1-11 _____

John 10:11 _____

5. Seeing the Father through Jesus and learning to relate to Him in a personal and intimate way is vital. Spend a few minutes thanking God for Who He is and what He is really like. Ask God to reveal Himself to you more clearly and enable you to have a deeper, more intimate relationship with Him. Remember that His ability and His desire to reveal Himself to you is greater than your ability and desire to see Him differently.

6. Continue to meditate on verses pertaining to God's character from Day Two.

The Truth About God - Day Four

Goal: To begin recognizing and receiving your Heavenly Father's thoughts towards you.

Many, O Lord my God, are the wonderful works which You have done, and Your thoughts toward us; no one can compare with You! If I should declare and speak of them, they are too many to be numbered. Psalm 40:5 Amplified

How precious and weighty also are Your thoughts to me, O God! How vast is the sum of them! If I could count them, they would be more in number than the sand. Psalm 139:17-18a Amplified

1. Read out loud the following paraphrased, personalized verses, placing your name in the blanks.

2. Meditate on one of these verses during the next few days. Receive this as your Heavenly Father's thoughts toward you each morning before you start your day and each night before you go to sleep.

MY HEAVENLY FATHER'S THOUGHTS TOWARD ME

For I AM the Lord! Your Lord, _____ , I AM merciful and gracious; slow to become angry and overflowing with lovingkindness and truth, maintaining lovingkindness toward you. I have forgiven your wickedness, rebellion and sin. Exodus 34:6

For the Spirit which you received (at the moment of new birth) is not a spirit of slavery to return you to bondage to fear; rather you have received from Me the Spirit of adoption! I have made you My child and in the bliss and security of that position, _____ you can cry "Abba" or "Father" (Daddy)! The Holy Spirit Himself witnesses to your spirit telling you this is so, assuring you that you are My child. Romans 8:15-16

_____, My child, do not dread, neither be afraid, for I AM the Lord your God (your Father) Who goes before you in your trouble; I will fight for you, just as I did the nation of Israel when I brought them out of Egypt. I will carry you just like I did them, just as a man carries his son. Deuteronomy 1:29-31

This is what I, the Lord Who created you, Who formed you says; Fear not, _____, for I have redeemed you. I have bought you back for Myself by paying the price of My life instead of leaving you captive. I have called you personally by name, and you are Mine. Therefore, when you walk through the waters of trouble, I, your Father, will be with you, and as you go through the rivers, they will not overwhelm you; when you walk through the fire you shall not be burned or scorched, nor shall the flame touch you. Fear not because I, your Father, am with you. You are precious in My sight, and honored, and I love you! Isaiah 43:1-4

Listen to Me, _____ , I the Lord, your Father, have borne you from your birth; I carried you from the womb. Even to your old age I will remain the same, for I AM the source of supply for your every need; even until your hair is white with age, I, your Father will carry you, _____ , and deliver you! Isaiah 46:3-4

And the Lord, your Father, declares to you: Can a woman forget her nursing child and have no compassion on the son of her womb? Yes, she may forget, yet your Father will not forget you, _____ . See, I have indelibly tattooed a picture of you on the palm of each of My hands. Isaiah 49:15-16

I, the Lord, your Father, have loved you, _____ , with a love that never ends; therefore, with My favor and merciful kindness I have taken the initiative and have drawn you to myself. Jeremiah 31:3

Fear not, _____, and don't let your hands sink down and don't be discouraged, for I AM with you in everything! I AM the Mighty One, the Savior Who saves! I AM rejoicing over you with joy! I rest in the silent satisfaction of your being My child and in the love that I have for you. I will never make mention of your past sins or even recall them. I delight in you and rejoice over you with singing! Zephaniah 3:16-17

Dear Child, I made you alive when you were dead in your sins; those sins in which you, at one time, walked habitually. You were then destined for my wrath like the rest of mankind. But I, being rich in mercy and in order to satisfy the great and wonderful and intense love that I have for you, made you alive together in fellowship and in union with My Son Jesus, by giving you His very life. All because of My grace and mercy, which you did not deserve, you have been delivered from My righteous judgment. Not only have I made you alive to Me, _____, but I have raised you up with Jesus and have seated you with Him in the heavenly sphere, by virtue of your being IN Christ Jesus. I did this for you to demonstrate clearly for all eternity the immeasurable, limitless, surpassing riches of My free grace, given to you out of the kindness and goodness of My heart. For it is by My free and gracious love that you have been delivered from judgment and made a partaker of My salvation in Christ, which you have received by faith. Always remember your salvation is not of your own doing; you did not obtain it by your own striving or performance, but it is a free gift from Me, your Heavenly Father. Ephesians 2:4-10

The Truth About God - Day Five

Goal: To understand how to live and walk as God's child.

1. Underline the important sentences that speak to you in this lesson. Write out the main idea or thought you received from the Lord.

2. Ask God to reveal to you who / what you have turned to to meet your deepest need. Fill in the blanks below.

   I have primarily depended upon _____ to meet my need for love. I have tried to _____ in order to feel like I belong. I have depended on _____ to give me a sense of well-being. I have depended upon _____ to make me feel secure. I have looked to _____ for approval. I have tried to gain acceptance from _____ by _____ I have worshiped (valued) _____ more than God.

3. Pray the following prayer out loud to God.

Dear Heavenly Father, I have come to realize that I do not know You as You really are, and because of this, I have not experienced the kind of intimacy that You desire to have with me. I have looked to myself, others, and things to meet my deepest needs. I now desire for You to meet these needs by interacting with You daily in a close and intimate way. I want to know You as fully as possible, but I don't know how to get to know You. So, Father, I'm asking You to reveal Yourself to me through Your Word and in my daily life. Open my eyes that I might see Your glory, majesty, and goodness. Open my mind and heart to understand and to receive Your perfect unconditional love for me.

The Truth About God - Lesson Four Summary

Name _____ Date _____

Answer the following questions. To turn in page to small group leader.

1. What corrupted beliefs about God as Father did you recognize through this lesson?

2. How would knowing and relating to God as your Father affect your life (emotionally, relationally, behaviorally)?

3. How would relating to God as an unconditionally loving and perfect Father affect your life?

4. What from this week's assignment was most meaningful to you?

5. What characteristic(s) of God need strengthening in your life?

6. Mark the graph to indicate how much of this week's assignment you completed.

None————————————————50%————————————————100%

The Truth About the Holy Spirit

But when He, the Spirit of truth, comes, He will guide you into all the truth; for He will not speak on His own initiative, but whatever He hears, He will speak; and He will disclose to you what is to come. He will glorify Me, for He will take of Mine and will disclose it to you.

John 16:13-14

Lesson Five

A Life Transformed....

My parents divorced when I was a baby. When my mother abandoned us, and my father couldn't take care of us, I was sent to a boarding school for Indian children when I was five years old. I felt like an orphan and as if I never belonged to anyone, especially when my brother and sister went to live with my mother for a while but I never did.

When I was 12 years old, I became a Christian, but nothing changed. I still felt lonely and unwanted, like an orphan, and I thought that God was distant and uncaring. No one told me that the Christian life would be different.

Many years later I learned that when I became a Christian, the Holy Spirit came to live in me. I realized that I had been living as if I had a dead spirit and as if I were still separated from God, as if I were still a spiritual orphan. I had read in John 14 that Jesus Christ said that the Holy Spirit would teach me, so I started asking the Holy Spirit, "Will you teach me about myself so that I can understand my life and know who I am?"

to be continued...

The Truth about the Holy Spirit
Lesson Five

The Person of the Holy Spirit

We have already discovered how our faulty beliefs about ourselves and about God affect the quality of our lives. This lesson will help us discover how to live life by the Spirit rather than by the flesh. We were created to contain the Spirit of God and to live by His life. Only as we live by the Spirit do we experience our new identity and enjoy a satisfying relationship with God. What are some facts concerning the Holy Spirit?

- God is revealed in three persons: Father, Son, and Holy Spirit. The Holy Spirit is identical in essence to God the Father and God the Son.
- He is a person, not an "it" or a "power."
- He has a mind (knows and communicates God's thoughts (1 Corinthians 2:10-11),
- He has a will (distributes gifts as He wills (1 Corinthians 12:11), and
- He has emotions (can be grieved - Ephesians 4:30), expresses joy (Luke 10:21).

The Holy Spirit is Christ living in us

Jesus promised to send the Holy Spirit to live in those who receive Him.

> *But the one who joins himself to the Lord is one spirit with Him.* 1 Corinthians 6:17 NASB

The word "one" in "one spirit" is the same word used for the "one flesh" relationship between husband and wife. The two shall become "one flesh" (Genesis 2:24) means that they no longer function as two separate, independent people. Likewise, we have become one with Christ's Spirit who is living through us.

> *. . . it is no longer I who live, but Christ lives in me; and the life which I now live in the flesh I live by faith in the Son of God . . .* Galatians 2:20b NASB

The Holy Spirit is our helper

In John 14:16, Jesus described the Holy Spirit as "another Helper," meaning another of the very same kind. The Holy Spirit is to us all that Jesus was to His disciples and more. He does for us what Jesus would do for us if He were physically present. He is our permanent resident Counselor, Comforter, Helper, Intercessor, Advocate, and Strengthener.

> *And I will ask the Father, and He will give you another Comforter (Counselor, Helper, Intercessor, Advocate, Strengthener, and Standby), that He may remain with you forever.* John 14:16 Amplified

The Holy Spirit is our comforter

Our Heavenly Father is the God of all comfort. He has given us His Spirit to comfort us as we experience life. We need God's comfort when we feel rejected, sad, lonely or depressed. We need God's comfort when we experience trials or when we lose a friend or loved one. God cares about how we feel and has not left us alone. The Holy Spirit allows us to hear God and receive His comfort.

Counselor

Helper

Intercessor

Revealer

Strengthener

Comforter

Teacher

Truth about Holy Spirit

Our behavior neither brings oneness with Him or separates us from Him.

His behavior brought us and keeps us in oneness with Him.

The Holy Spirit is our teacher

Jesus has not left us to figure out life on our own. He has given us the Holy Spirit to teach us the truth about God, ourselves, life and others. He not only teaches us but also He reminds us of the truth. He gives us God's perspective, wisdom, and understanding. Remember: Learning requires listening and attention.

> *But the Comforter (Counselor, Helper, Intercessor, Advocate, Strengthener, Standby), the Holy Spirit, Whom the Father will send in My name [in My place, to represent Me and act on My behalf], He will teach you all things. And He will cause you to recall (will remind you of, bring to your remembrance) everything I have told you.* John 14:26 Amplified

LIFE IN THE SPIRIT

> *"I do not pray for these alone, but also for those who will believe in Me through their word; that they all may be one, as You, Father, are in Me, and I in You; that they also may be one in Us, that the world may believe that You have sent Me. And the glory which You gave Me I have given them, that they may be one just as We are one: I in them, and You in Me; that they may be made perfect in one, and that the world may know that You have sent Me, and have loved them as You have loved Me."*

John 17:20-23 NKJV.

This prayer was fulfilled by Holy Spirit being given to us. Holy Spirit in us is the One who bestows on us the gift of Oneness with God, He is the "glory" given to us, and He is also the One who reminds us of the truth we are loved by God as He loves Jesus.

The Oneness we have been given will never change. We live and move and have our being in Holy Spirit. We are always in the Spirit! Walking after the flesh will not change our oneness, no disobedience, nothing will separate us from the oneness given to us. Our choice to walk according to the flesh, disobedience of any kind will only make us miserable, harm us and others, but it will NOT take us out of the Spirit. It was not our good behavior that brought us into oneness and our behavior cannot take us out.

> *For I am persuaded that neither death nor life, nor angels nor principalities nor powers, nor things present nor things to come, nor height nor depth, nor any other created thing, shall be able to separate us from the love of God which is in Christ Jesus our Lord.* Romans 8:37-39 NKJV.

Living by and relying on the Spirit is essential to experience intimacy with God and expressing all we already are in Christ. It is important to realize and remember:

- *I am the sprouting vine and you're my branches. As you live in union with me as your source, fruitfulness will stream from within you—but when you live separated from me you are powerless.* John 15:5 TPT.

Copyright 1998, 2001, 2005, 2007, 2019, 2020   Scope Ministries International, INC.

- *as His divine power has given to us all things that pertain to life and godliness, through the knowledge of Him who calls us by glory and virtue.* 2 Peter 1:3 NKJV.

Living by the Spirit is ceasing from our works and resting in His life and power flowing through us. Jesus promised this would be like "rivers of living water."

If any man is thirsty, let him come to Me and drink. He who believes in Me, as the Scripture said, "From his innermost being shall flow rivers of living water." But this He spoke of the Spirit, whom those who believed in Him were to receive; for the Spirit was not yet given, because Jesus was not yet glorified. John 7:37b-39 NASB.

This kind of life is described as Sabbath Rest found in Hebrews 4:9.

There remains, then, a Sabbath-rest for the people of God; for anyone who enters God's rest also rests from their works, just as God did from his. NIV.

Being Filled With the Spirit

We were filled with Holy Spirit when we first experienced Christ as Savior. There are at least 2 Greek words for filled. One is *plesoo* and means "filled inwardly (for life), satisfy." The other is *pletho* and means furnished and equipped "filled outwardly, accomplished (for ministry)". They also have the meaning of:

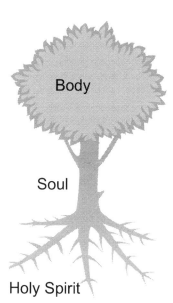

Body (*Bios Life*): Produces a transformed life in the fruit of the Spirit.

Soul (*Psuche Life*): Reveals truth to our minds.. Fills us with love, joy and peace. Motivates us to do God's will.

Spirti *(Zoe Life)*: Christ in Us.

We have already been given everything we need for life and Godliness through the presence of the Holy Spirit in our spirit. This is the mystery of the Gospel; Christ in us, the hope of glory (Colossians 1:27) The tree illustrates the ministry of the Holy Spirit in the soul of a believer. What the Holy Spirit has done for us produces a change in our behavior.

> *Do not try to improve the flesh or get rid of the flesh, live and walk in the Spirit by faith allowing Him to change you.*

Truth about Holy Spirit

A Spirit-filled life is a moment-by-moment relationship with Jesus. It is like a ballroom dance. The Holy Spirit leads and we follow,

abounding, abundant, ample, complete, perfect, to satisfy. Taken from Spiros Zodhiates, *The Complete Word Study New Testament*.

A picture for being filled inward for life and outward for ministry is the river in the garden of Eden. There was one river that flowed out of Eden and became four river heads. (See Genesis 2:10)

We are filled once for life. Out of that filling will flow rivers of living water to minister Christ's life to others.

Jesus promised never to leave us nor forsake us. He promised to live in and through us by His Spirit. The Spirit satisfies our spirit and soul. He has furnished to us everything needed for life and godliness. He promised to fill our hunger and thirst for righteousness.

> *Blessed are they which do hunger and thirst after righteousness: for they shall be filled.* Matthew 5:6 NASB.

Jesus abundantly and perfectly, accomplished this promise by giving us His life and His righteousness by the Spirit.

As we live dependent on Holy Spirit, we are being filled and satisfied and are focused on receiving, relating, and responding to God. It is like a ballroom dance. The Holy Spirit leads and we follow. The Holy Spirit prompts us in our thoughts and we simply respond, believing He will empower us to do God's will. This is a moment-by-moment relationship that will leave us satisfied and fulfilled.

Choosing the Truth

The memory of our old way of living independent of Holy Spirit still influences us on a daily basis. Our old ways of thinking, old habits and emotional responses are very familiar to us. At first the thoughts and ways of the Spirit can seem foreign. Even the Apostle Paul had to learn not to put confidence in his old ways (flesh).

Many believers unknowingly allow the flesh to determine their identity. As Christians, our identity is NOT in our flesh, but in our spirit. Jesus said that the flesh profits nothing, but the Spirit gives life.

> *It is the Spirit who gives life; the flesh profits nothing; the words that I have spoken to you are spirit and are life.* John 6:63, NASB

> *However, you are not in the flesh but in the Spirit, if indeed the Spirit of God dwells in you.* Romans 8:9a NASB

We are tempted to rely on our own abilities and strengths.

> *But I say, walk by the Spirit, and you will not carry out the desire of the flesh. For the flesh sets its desire against the Spirit, and the Spirit against the flesh; for these are in opposition to one another, so that you may not do the things that you please.* Galatians 5:16-17 NASB

Living by the flesh is trying to meet our needs apart from God. The flesh can appear good and respectable, but it can never produce God's quality of life.

> *But the fruit of the Spirit is love, joy, peace, patience, kindness, goodness, faithfulness, gentleness, self-control; against such things there is no law.* Galatians 5:22-23 NASB

Copyright 1998, 2001, 2005, 2007, 2019, 2020 Scope Ministries International, INC.

We can attempt to produce the "fruit of the Spirit" (love, joy, peace, patience, kindness goodness, faithfulness, gentleness, and self-control) through our own self-effort. Attempting to produce the fruit of the Spirit by relying on our own abilities and strengths is similar to tying fruit on a tree. The fruit of the Spirit is produced from *Zoe* life not *psuche* life or *bios* life. The fruit can be revealed through our soul and body but does not originate from them.

Truth about Holy Spirit

The following chart will help to see the difference between the flesh walk and the Spirit walk.

Spirit Walk	Flesh Walk
Relate to Jesus by faith John 7:37-38; Colossians 2:6	Rely on self and others Jeremiah 17:5-6
Trust in the character of God Proverbs 3:5-6; Jeremiah 24:7	See God in an inaccurate way Romans 1:25; 1 Corinthians 15:34
Praise and thank God Ephesians 5:18-19; Psalms; Hebrews 13:15	Pessimistic, discontent, and ungrateful Romans 1:21; James 4:14,16
Consideration and love for others Ephesians 5:21; Romans 12:10	Act envious, jealous, selfish 1 Corinthians 3:3; James 4:1-2
Request God's wisdom 1 Corinthians 2:10-13; James 1:5	Rely on own understanding Isaiah 55:8-9; 1 Corinthians 1:27; 3:18-20;
Believe my new identity 2 Corinthians 5:17; Colossians 3:10	Believe my old identity Ephesians 4:22; Colossians 3:9
Security in my relationship with God Romans 8:16; Galatians 4:7-8	Lack assurance of salvation 1 John 2:28-29; 1 John 4:17
Abide in God's love Romans 5:5; Ephesians 3:16-19; 1 John 3:1	Fear God's punishment 1 John 4:18; 1 John 2:28
Rest in God's acceptance Romans 15:7; Ephesians 1:4	Work for God's acceptance Galatians 2:16, 21; Galatians 5:1-6
Trust Christ to live through me Matthew 11:18-20; Hebrews 4:10	Strive to do good in my own strength Romans 7; Galatians 3:2-3; Colossians 2:20-23
Rely on the Holy Spirit to teach John 14:26; John 16:13	Rely on my own ability to learn John 5:38-40; 1 Corinthians 8:1-2
Acknowledge God's presence and activity in my daily life. 2 Corinthians 4:18; Hebrews 11:6	Do not recognize God's involvement in my daily life Romans 1:28; Hebrews 3:7-10
Base my worth on who Christ has made me to be Philippians 2:5-6; James 4:10; 1 Peter 5:6	Base worth on performance, appearance, and others' opinions Jeremiah 9:23-24; Romans 12:16; James 4:5-6

Truth about Holy Spirit

> *The Spirit-filled life is about God getting more of you, not you getting more of God!*

We cannot produce fruit by self-effort. The Holy Spirit grows His fruit in us as we walk by faith in Him.

> *Remain in [continue to believe and rely on] Me, and I will remain in [dwell and fill] you. No branch can bear fruit by itself; it must remain in the vine. Neither can you bear fruit unless you remain in Me. . . You did not choose Me, but I chose you and appointed you to go and bear fruit—fruit that will last.*
> John 15:4, 16 Amplified

Transformation occurs through living by the Spirit, not by improving our flesh.

Living by the Spirit is a radically different way of life. It is much more than changing our behavior. It is learning to live moment-by-moment by faith in Christ's life within us. His life will ultimately change our behavior.

Being filled with the Holy Spirit does not mean we will never struggle with faulty beliefs, emotions, or behvaiors. It does mean that we will live in a vital and personal relationship with God and will allow Jesus to live through our soul and body (Galatians 2:20). As a result others are touched by His presence in our lives,

> *We choose to walk relying on the Holy Spirit.*

Summary:

1. He comes to live in us at salvation and will never leave or forsake us. He is our Helper, Comforter, Teacher, and Friend.

2. To be filled by the Spirit means to be motivated, led, and empowered by the Holy Spirit, allowing Him to live through us.

3. Daily, we walk by faith is all that God has provided in Him.

4. Spiritual life is a moment-by-moment relationship with Jesus, relying on the Holy Spirit to lead and empower us in our daily lives.

A Life Transformed, con't.

One day while I was driving and enjoying the beautiful clouds, the Holy Spirit told me, "Ruby, you are a child of God. That's who you are." He showed me that I am loved and very special to Him. He showed me that I am free from the bondage of my wrong belief that I am an orphan. That was the beginning of understanding my identity in Christ and the beginning of a relationship with God that is more than knowing that I'll go to heaven when I die.

The Holy Spirit has changed me. I used to be really quiet and withdrawn, and I didn't want people around me because I thought that if they knew me they wouldn't want me. Now I am more outgoing and confident and joyful because I'm not as afraid of rejection as I used to be. I know who I am in Christ, and I know that He loves me unconditionally regardless of my mistakes.

The Holy Spirit has taught me. When I first started co-leading small group studies, I depended upon the other leader in the group to help me because I believed that I wasn't smart enough to do it by myself. The first time I had to lead a group by myself, I thought, "I can't do this because I don't understand the material. I'm not living it." The Holy Spirit responded, "Yes, you do, and yes, you are." I know that the Holy Spirit speaks only the truth, so I was really excited to realize that I truly do understand the material.

Another time I asked the Holy Spirit to show me a wrong belief in my life. He brought to my mind a scene from the movie Annie. She's in a room with a long row of beds, much like the boarding school where I grew up. Annie thought that she had to be tough and take care of herself. The Holy Spirit showed me that this is how I used to be: tough — so that I wouldn't feel emotions — and really independent from God. I was so encouraged when God showed me how much I've changed.

The Holy Spirit is changing how I interact with my children. He showed me that it's not my job to change them. I have a daughter who's married to an alcoholic who verbally abuses her. I used to get angry with her and tell her that she didn't need a husband like that. By not accepting her, I alienated her and my grandchildren because she didn't want to tell me what was going on in their lives when she knew I wouldn't like it.

Now the Holy Spirit is enabling me to give her the freedom to make her choices and to accept her unconditionally, and she's beginning to trust me more. I'm no longer trying to control the situation, but it is still an area of my life that's hard, and I have to depend constantly on the Spirit. I tell Him, "You know how I used to be. I need you to remind me when I start withdrawing from her that I don't have to be that way anymore."

Through the Holy Spirit, I am experiencing the joy, freedom, and love that God has for me. He interacts with me in the most personal ways, and the more I know God, as He really is, the more I want to be with Him. The more I am with Him, the more I become like Him. That's the very best work of the Spirit!

Ruby - Biblical Personal Guidance Minister

The Truth about the Holy Spirit - Day One

Goal: To understand the person of the Holy Spirit.

The Holy Spirit is God within us. He is more than a "power." He is a person Who has a mind (knows and communicates God's thoughts), a will (distributes gifts as He wills—1 Corinthians 12:11), and emotions (can be grieved, made sorrowful—Ephesians 4:30). He is called the "Spirit of Truth" in John 5:26.

1. In John 14:26, what is the Holy Spirit called?

2. In John 15:26, what is the Holy Spirit called?

3. Who is sending Him?

4. In Romans 8:2, what is the Holy Spirit called?

5. How does Isaiah 11:2 describe the Holy Spirit?

6. Galatians 5:22-23 lists some of the fruit of the Spirit. What emotions does this list indicate that the Holy Spirit has?

7. Write each of the nine characteristics of the fruit of the Spirit out in this manner:

    1) The Holy Spirit is love.

    2)

    3)

    4)

    5)

    6)

    7)

    8)

    9)

8. Based on what you've just read about the Holy Spirit, write your own description of Who the Holy Spirit is to you personally.

9. Is this the type of person you could trust? Why or why not?

10. According to 1 Corinthians 6:19, what is your body?

11. According to Romans 12:1, what are you to do?

12. Ask the Lord to reveal Himself through the Holy Spirit.

Ask Him to remind you of His ever-present life within.

The Truth about the Holy Spirit - Day Two

Goal: To understand the Holy Spirit's role in your life.

1. What does John 6:63 tell us the Spirit does?

2. According to John 14:17, where does the Holy Spirit live?

3. Read the following verses and write what the Holy Spirit will do for you.

    a) John 14:26

    b) John 16:13

    c) Romans 5:5

    d) Romans 8:15

    e) Romans 8:16

    f) Romans 8:27

    g) Romans 15:13

4. Read John 15:1-5. The word "abide" means to dwell or make yourself at home. Abiding in Jesus is simply giving oneself to Him to be ruled and taught and led, thereby resting in His unconditional love. According to verse 4 and 5, how much of the Christian life can you accomplish on your own?

5. In what ways have you tried to live the Christian life on your own?

6. Write down some personal examples of how the Holy Spirit has been working in your life until now (reflect on your answers to question 3).

7. Write a thank-you note to the Holy Spirit, expressing your gratitude for all He has already done for you.

The Truth about the Holy Spirit - Day Three

Goal: To recognize your need to walk by faith and depend moment-by-moment on the Holy Spirit.

Jesus described the Spirit-filled life as thirsting and drinking and walking. Each of these activities is repetitive in nature.

> *If we live by the Spirit, let us also walk by the Spirit.* Galatians 5:25 NASB

> *As you have therefore received Christ . . . so walk in Him.* Colossians 2:6 NASB

1. How did you receive Christ? How are you to walk?

2. We exercise faith in Christ not only at salvation but also daily, moment-by-moment. With each new situation or need, we express faith in Christ, Who is our life. Read Galatians 2:20. How does Paul say he now lives?

3. Read John 7:37-39. Thirst expresses our continuous need and desire to know God. How often during a day do you get thirsty? How often do you think of trusting Jesus?

4. The following verses express the psalmist's longing for God. Write your own psalm expressing your thirst to God.

> *As the deer pants for the water brooks, So my soul longs for Thee, O God.*
> *My soul thirsts for God, for the living God.* Psalm 42:1-2a, NASB

5. Drinking expresses receiving by faith. Every time we are thirsty (long for God) we acknowledge His presence (by talking to Him).

> *If any man is thirsty, let him come to Me and drink. He who believes in Me, as the Scripture said, 'From his innermost being shall flow rivers of living water.'* John 7:37b-38 NASB

6. Read John 4:5-24 about Jesus and the Samaritan woman. How was the woman trying to satisfy her thirst (her inward needs)? What did Jesus offer her?

7. Read John 5:38-40. Jesus was addressing the religious leaders who knew the Scriptures well. In fact, they had memorized most of it. What were these religious people missing? Why?

8. How have you tried to satisfy your thirst? (relationships, approval of others, material possessions, job, fame, etc.)

9. Write Galatians 2:20, personalizing it and putting it into your own words.

10. Express to Jesus your desire to trust Him moment by moment to satisfy your deepest needs and desires.

The Truth about the Holy Spirit - Day Four

Goal: To understand the value of living by the Spirit.

Living by the flesh is simply living by our own natural abilities, energy, and strength to meet our needs apart from God. Although the flesh might even appear very good and respectable, it can never produce God's quality of life.

After God promised Sarah and Abraham a son, Sarah persuaded Abraham to father a child by her handmaid, Hagar. This produced Ishmael, who persecuted Isaac, the son promised by God. These two sons represent the difference between living by the flesh and living by the Spirit.

1. Read Galatians 4:22-24; 28-29. Ishmael represents depending on our own energy, natural ability and strength. Isaac, the son of promise, represents the supernatural life of the Spirit. In what ways have you tried to fulfill God's plan for your life through your own energy, natural ability, and strength?

2. Through the life of the Apostle Peter, we can see the contrast between the flesh and the Spirit. Before the Holy Spirit was given, Peter was earnest in his efforts to follow Christ, but all his human effort ended in his denying Christ. Read Matthew 26:26, 31-35.

3. After the Holy Spirit was given on the day of Pentecost, Peter courageously and boldly proclaimed the Gospel. Even when experiencing physical suffering and persecution, Peter rejoiced in the Lord and continued to proclaim Him to others. Read Acts 4:13; 5:27-29.

4. Read Philippians 3:3-6. Describe the Apostle Paul's flesh.

5. Read John 6:63. What did Jesus say about the Spirit and the flesh?

6. Read 1 Corinthians 2:7-13. What does the Spirit reveal to your mind?

7. Looking back over today's answers, what personal benefit do you think you would receive by being motivated, led, and empowered by the Holy Spirit?

8. How would living by the Spirit change you during your present struggles and how you view your present circumstances?

9. In what areas do you need to receive God's wisdom?

10. In what areas do you need to receive God's strength?

11. In what ways do you need to be comforted by God?

12. Spend some time thanking God for being your resident Counselor, Teacher, Comforter, Helper, and Strengthener. Ask Him to remind you of how He has been all of these to you in the past. Ask Him to make you more aware of His presence in the future.

The Truth about the Holy Spirit - Day Five

Goal: To recognize wrong beliefs that hinder you from experiencing a Spirit-filled life.

1. According to the following verse, what is God's will concerning how you are to walk?

   Therefore be careful how you walk, not as unwise men, but as wise, making the most of your time, because the days are evil. So then do not be foolish but understand what the will of the Lord is. And do not get drunk with wine, for that, but is dissipation but be [continually] filled with the Spirit. Ephesians 5:15-18, NASB

2. Read Galatians 2:20. Ask Him to begin teaching you how to live by faith in the Spirit.

3.. Read the chart on page 133, "Common Wrong Beliefs About the Spirit-filled Life." Write out the wrong beliefs that best represent your thinking, then read the corresponding truth and Scriptures.

4. Choose to put off the lies you have believed about the Spirit and replace them with the truth based on Scripture. Ask the Holy Spirit to remind you when the lies influence your thoughts again.

5. Read the following verses, then take a few minutes to express to God your decision to yield control of your life to Him and to be filled with His Spirit.

Or do you not know that your body is a temple of the Holy Spirit who is in you, whom you have from God, and that you are not your own? For you have been bought with a price: therefore, glorify God in your body.
1 Corinthians 6:19-20 NASB

But if the Spirit of Him who raised Jesus from the dead dwells in you, He who raised Christ Jesus from the dead will also give life to your mortal bodies through His Spirit who indwells you. So then, brethren, we are under obligation, not to the flesh, to live according to the flesh—for if you are living according to the flesh, you must die; but if by the Spirit you are putting to death the deeds of the body, you will live. Romans 8:11-13 NASB

Common Wrong Beliefs About the Spirit-filled Life

Lie	Truth
I live my life with God as my helper. I can't expect God to do everything. Implication: God helps those who help themselves.	God wants to live His life through me by means of the Spirit. He says that I can do NOTHING apart from Him! John 15:5; Acts 17:28; Galatians 2:20
I can control my life better than the Holy Spirit. If I let the Spirit control my life, then my life would be out of control Implication: My control is better than God's control.	When I try to control my life, I actually become out of control. Living by my laws and standards activates the principle of sin, and I inevitably end up doing the opposite of what I want to do. By allowing the Spirit to live through me, I am empowered with self-control. Romans 7:4, 8, 15; Galatians 5:16, 22-23; 2 Timothy 1:7
Living by faith in the Holy Spirit is foreign to me, unnatural, contrary to how I best operate. Implication: God is unwise and doesn't know what is best for me.	I am primarily a spiritual being. Living by faith in the Spirit is consistent with who I really am. Living by faith may feel awkward initially because it has not been the way I have been living my life. However, God calls me to walk by the Spirit because He knows that is how I have been designed by Him to live. It is how I best operate. Romans 8:14-16; Galatians 2:20
If I submit to the Spirit, I'll have to give up _____. I won't enjoy life as much. Implication: God doesn't know or care about my desires. He may withhold something from me that I really want and that would be terrible. My enjoyment in life is based on external things.	Fullness of joy comes from knowing God and living conscious of His presence. The Holy Spirit enables me to experience and know God intimately, which results in unequaled joy and peace. My Heavenly Father cares about my needs and desires. He delights in giving to me and is infinitely wise in knowing the perfect gifts and perfect time to give those gifts to me. Psalm 16:11; Matthew 7:7-11; Romans 8:31-32; James 1:17
The Spirit-filled life is unclear and confusing. I cannot live by the Spirit; it is too hard. Implication: God is telling me to do something and not telling me how to do it. He is unclear and confusing.	God is not a God of confusion, but of peace. He commands me to be filled with the Spirit, and His commandments are not burdensome. God desires more than I do that I learn to live and walk by the Spirit. I can trust Him to teach me and clarify the truth to me. Matthew 11:28-30; 1 Corinthians 14:33; Ephesians 5:18; 1 John 5:3
I will be obnoxiously over-spiritual, do crazy-looking things, and alienate people if I am filled with the Spirit. Implication: God will make me weird and obnoxious.	The Holy Spirit is God. God is not obnoxious, overly pushy, or insensitive to people. He desires to draw people to Himself, not alienate them. The Spirit lives uniquely through the personality of each person. The Holy Spirit is in the process of conforming all of us to the image of Jesus; therefore, comparing ourselves to others is non-productive. 1 Corinthians 13:4-8; 2 Corinthians 3:18, 10:12

The Roles of the Holy Spirit

Imparts Life — (John 6:63) The Holy Spirit gives us Eternal Life, which is God's quality of life. He has given us everything we need to live life to its fullest. The Holy Spirit has deposited God's resurrection life in our spirit. When we live by the Spirit, we experience God's quality of life.

Imparts Hope — (Romans 15:13) The Holy Spirit is God's active agent for change. He is the "down payment," assuring us that God will complete the good work He started in us through the regenerating work of the Holy Spirit.

Imparts Spiritual Gifts — (Romans 12:5-8) The Holy Spirit has given spiritual gifts to each believer so that they are equipped to minister to others.

Reveals Truth — (John 16:13) The Holy Spirit guides us into all truth. Truth taught by the Holy Spirit is the unveiling of the unseen reality. He longs to do this because the truth will set us free (John 8:32).

Reveals Jesus — (John 16:14) The Holy Spirit makes Christ real to us. Anyone can learn information about Jesus, but only the Holy Spirit can make Jesus known to us in a personal, intimate way.

Reveals God's Thoughts — (1 Corinthians 2:10-13) The Holy Spirit puts God's thoughts in our minds and reveals to us the things freely given to us by God. Since we have the mind of Christ, we can receive God's wisdom for daily living. The Holy Spirit makes an intimate relationship with God possible.

Reveals God's Love — (Romans 5:5; John 4:8-10, 18-19) The Holy Spirit makes God's love known to us. Only as we experience His unconditional love are we freed from fear and able to trust His ways. The more God's love is revealed to us by the Holy Spirit, the more we love God.

Reveals Things to Come — (John 16:13) At times the Holy Spirit even shows us what lies ahead, preparing us for future events. The Holy Spirit gives us practical guidance in our daily lives.

Empowers Us With Supernatural Life — (Ephesians 1:17-20; 3:16) The Holy Spirit empowers us to face all of life's obstacles with confidence and hope. He empowers us to rejoice in our trials and to love the most difficult people. The Holy Spirit gives us spiritual gifts to empower us to serve and minister to others.

Empowers Us to Love Others — (Galatians 5:22) The Holy Spirit is God and God is love, therefore, the fruit of the Spirit is love. The Holy Spirit empowers us to do what God commands: to love one another as He has loved us.

The Truth about the Holy Spirit - Lesson Five Summary

Name _____ Date _____

Answer the following questions. To turn in page to small group leader, use identical perforated page in back of book.

1. What encouraged you most about this week's study on the Holy Spirit?

2. List any fears or concerns you have about surrendering control of your life to the Holy Spirit.

3. What do you feel would keep God from filling you with His Spirit?

4. How would living by the Spirit affect your life and your current struggles?

5. Mark the graph to indicate how much of this week's assignment you completed.

0 %————————————————50%————————————————

Freedom with Emotions

These things I remember, and I pour out my soul within me... Why are you in despair, O my soul? And why have you become disturbed within me? Hope in God, for I shall again praise Him for the help of His presence.
Psalm 42:4a, 5 NASB

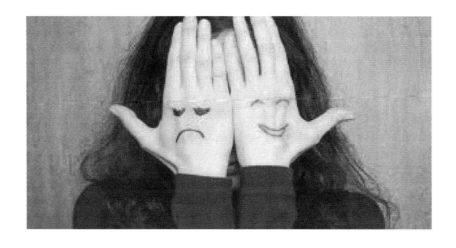

Lesson Six

A Life Transformed

When I was a child, my family didn't communicate well. Because my mother and father had marriage problems, my mom was usually depressed. When I was mad or sad, she would walk away while I was talking to her or send me to my room. I learned that it didn't do any good to express my emotions. I bottled them up inside and became emotionally numb.

Things got even worse in high school when my family experienced some tragedies. All of us had problems but no one ever talked about anything. My mother always said, "Talk only about good things," so we were silent instead. That was when my emotions really went crazy and I tried to suppress them. Instead they dominated my life. I escaped the hurt at home through drugs, guys, school, and performance. I was really depressed and sick a lot, so I tried to do things to feel better, but I never really dealt with my emotions.

I thought that God was just like my parents and didn't really care. When I first became a Christian in college I found that He really does care. It was a very emotional time because I started expressing myself to God. I cried out to Him a lot, and I felt relieved to tell Him everything. After a few rough times, though, I returned to my old pattern of suppressing my emotions. The more I tried ignoring them, the more they controlled me. I turned to some of the things I had done in the past to make myself feel better.

to be continued...

Freedom with Emotions
Lesson Six

When renewing our minds, one of the greatest obstacles we may encounter is emotion. Our society prizes feeling good and sees little value in emotional struggle. We may have been taught some emotions are 'good' and some are 'bad.' When we label them as such, we begin to see emotion as an entity, something that exists independently with no connection to anything else.

The Bible is filled with examples of both pleasant and unpleasant or "less acceptable" feelings. In this lesson we will learn more about our emotions, ways to express them and problems that may occur when they are mishandled. The goal is not to control our emotions but instead to recognize when they are controlling us.

Why Are We Emotional?

Emotional by design

God shows us throughout the Bible we are not meant to hide or ignore feelings. God is a spiritual Being Who expresses Himself emotionally. He openly allows us to know of His grief, anger, joy, excitement, love and compassion - John 4:24; Genesis 6:6; Psalm 106:40; Zephaniah 3:17; Isaiah 54:10. Jesus became human and continued to express Himself emotionally. He was angry when He drove the moneychangers from the Temple. He felt compassion toward the multitude who had been without food for three days. He was anxious in Gethsemane as He prepared for the cross. Because we are made in His image, we also, have the ability to feel a wide range of emotions.

Emotions are part of our soul

The soul is a magnificent creation of Father God which allows us to operate in the complex world created for us. In every small moment, we are taking in enormous amounts of information through our senses. We interpret that information within our soul coming up with ideas, thoughts and actions that lead to interactions with other people who are engaged in the same process. Through these experiences we live, learn, and form beliefs.

Each part of our soul is necessary. Our mind, which houses reason, interprets circumstances and information while stimulating emotional responses. These emotions can inspire more thoughts and deepen our understanding as conclusions and opinions are formed. The will does not make decisions without the presence of reason and emotion. Simply put, all the parts of our soul (thinking, feeling, choosing) must be engaged to relate to the world and people around us. This is part of our intricately woven design. As children of God, we learn to recognize Holy Spirit's involvement in this process.

Emotions are messengers

Imagine yourself on the highway when the oil light on your dashboard lights up. Do you ignore it and keep driving your car for the next few days? Do you reach into the glove box, pull out a screwdriver and disconnect the light so you don't have to see it anymore? Do you pull into a service station and ask the attendant to repair your light? No! The problem is not the light. The warning light is a messenger telling you about a deeper problem in the engine. The engine is what needs your attention; the light makes you aware of that need.

This is a great illustration to help us understand emotions are messengers of our internal beliefs about God, self, and others. Most people seek counseling because they are unhappy, frustrated, depressed, or anxious. Their emotions are telling them there is something "wrong" that needs to be acknowledged and addressed. Emotions alert us to look at underlying thoughts, beliefs and perceptions which may be faulty. When we become aware of a problem, we can then seek a solution; new ways to think, believe, and perceive life which are based on the truth of God's Word.

Emotions are morally neutral

Emotions are not good or bad. They are neutral indicators of what we think and believe. Some of us have been taught anger is a sin or that 'good Christians' don't feel angry. Ephesians 4:26 says *"Be angry yet do not sin."* Anger is not sin but the way we react to our emotions may cause us to act wrongly. Emotions can reveal an area where we are believing lies about our self or God. Responding to these lies can cause us to behave irrationally and feel emotionally out of control as we shift into survival mode and attempt to meet our own needs apart from God. Most graciously, God does not turn His face away from us when we feel overcome by "negative" emotions. God never condemns or belittles us because of our struggles. Both pleasant and unpleasant emotions are a normal part of the Christian life. God goes with us in our difficulty and does not leave or become disappointed when it takes a long time for us to see His sufficiency.

Characteristics of Emotion

Emotions are intended to be helpful

Emotions powerfully influence our desire to change or receive change. Curiosity or enjoyment of a subject may inspire us to seek more information and explore new directions. Anger or discontentment can

Copyright 1998, 2001, 2005, 2007, 2019, 2020 Scope Ministries International, INC.

motivate us to change an unjust law. Fear of failing or having to repeat a class may prompt us to study.

Emotional pain is to our soul what physical pain is to our body. CIPA (Congenital Insensitivity to Pain with Anhydrosis) is a rare condition where a person is born unable to feel physical pain, heat or cold. You can imagine the extreme danger for a child who felt no reaction to injury or temperature! While pain serves a vital purpose we would not wish it on ourselves or others. Likewise, emotional pain has purpose. It warns us of a problem, so we can take action.

Ignoring physical pain can create significant problems. If we disregard a toothache, the tooth could become abscessed and poison the bloodstream. In the same way, if we refuse to address our emotional pain it will start to affect many seemingly unrelated areas of our life. Pain, whether physical or emotional, prompts us to seek out the cause and take steps to deal with it before it becomes worse.

Emotions enable us to enjoy God and the life He gives

Emotion heightens our experience and performance. Athletes may use self-talk or music to pump themselves up before a game. When directed well, the emotions produced can enhance their skills and performance. Actors and musicians pour feelings into their work so the audience is emotionally drawn into the experience and enjoyment is amplified. Emotions are so fully a part of our memories that we often remember how we felt more strongly than the details of an event.

Through emotion we express who we are in Christ. As we grow in our knowing of Jesus we respond to and reflect Him more naturally. Knowing and loving God involves our whole being. Before it is expressed outwardly, His character is experienced intellectually and emotionally within as He lives through us. We share in His same ability to feel grief, distress, and other unpleasant emotions, but also love, compassion, mercy, joy, and peace.

Emotions remind us to interact and relate with God

When our emotions send a message about a problem, we may try to fix the situation ourselves. We may not want to bother God with "small" matters or think we don't need Him for this circumstance. We may fear His discipline or believe He expects us to handle things on our own. There could be any number of reasons we choose to exclude God, but all are based on error. The truth, Jesus says, is we can do nothing apart from Him. We need God for every detail in life because He is Life. God cares how we feel, what we think, what we believe and how we interpret the circumstances of life.

Casting the whole of your care [all your anxieties, all your worries, all your concerns, once and for all] on Him, for He cares for you affectionately and cares about you watchfully. 1 Peter 5:7 AMPC

Anxiety and fear are meant to protect us by indicating danger. When they are present in the absence of a potentially harmful situation, they show us our emotions are reacting to something false. Faith does not mean we will never experience fear. Faith reminds us what action to take when fear and worry overcome us. We ask Father God where He is in this situation. We can trust Him to come alongside us everytime we experience these unwanted emotions. We can ask him to help us look beyond where we are and see where He is.

Guilt results in thinking "I've done wrong!"

Shame is "Something is wrong with me!.

Possible Implications of Emotions
Anxiety and fear are meant to protect us by indicating danger. When they are present in the absence of a potentially harmful situation, they show us our emotions are reacting to something false. Faith does not mean we will never experience fear. Faith reminds us what action to take when fear and worry overcome us. We ask Father God where He is in this situation. We can trust Him to come alongside us every time we experience these unwanted emotions. We can ask him to help us look beyond where we are and see where He is. For the One Who is perfect Love has promised, "I will never, no never, leave you nor forsake you." 1 John 4:16-18; Hebrews 13:5b
Shame indicates we are believing a lie that says what we have done is more powerful than what Christ has done. Shame says our value is diminished by our own behavior or the behavior of others towards us. It reminds us to seek truth which says our worth is established by Christ Who loves us and gave Himself up for us. In Christ, we have a new and secure identity. We are justified, reconciled, and saved by His work not our own. Our significance is anchored in the One Who is the same yesterday, today, and forever. It is only as we look into His face that we accurately see who we are and what we are worth. Galatians 2:20; 2 Corinthians 5:17; Romans 5:1, 18, 6:4-6; Hebrews 6:19, 13:8
Inadequacy or fear of failure reminds us that apart from our indwelling Lord we can do nothing. We are created for a dependent relationship—as little children—and we must rely on our Father's infinite wisdom and strength. John 15:3-5; Romans 8:14-15; Psalm 46:1; James 1:5
Loneliness tells us a need has not been perceptively met. It reminds us of our most vital need of intimate companionship which cannot be met in any other than our Father God. Loneliness can exist when a person is alone or surrounded by people. It is the call of our soul to reach out and be known. Known by our Creator, the Healer of the broken-hearted. He longs to reveal Himself to the lonely. Psalm 25:16-20; Psalm 68:5-6a; Psalm 147:3; Ephesians 2:4-5; Isaiah 30:18; Jerimiah 9:24, 29:13, 31:34; John 17:3
Anger is a messenger, reminding us that we live in a fallen world and life is not fair. It reminds us of our need to release God's mercy and forgiveness to others, yielding our rights and expectations to God, Who works everything together for our good. John 16:33; Ephesians 4:26-27; Hebrews 12:15; Philippians 2:5-8; Romans 8:28

Messy Emotions

Our emotions can be messy when they seem more true to us than what God says is true. They can disrupt our lives when we allow them to control us. Our emotions are messy when they become the final authority determining our behavior and beliefs.

Sin has affected us emotionally

Before man experienced sin, his emotions expressed the heart of his Creator. As Adam received revelation from God, his thoughts and emotions reflected on this Truth and he experienced the peace of God. When man's relationship with God changed due to sin, his mind became darkened, and his thoughts no longer reflected the truth about God. This gave rise to emotions such as fear, anger, guilt, and sadness. Living independently of God's truth, man's reason and emotions became his final authority for what he would believe. Because we have all been affected by sin, we often allow our emotions to control our beliefs and behavior.

When we act and react based on how we feel about what is happening in our lives, our emotions become the primary influence in our life, overriding God's Word and causing us to act contrary to who we are in Christ. Here are a few examples:

- I am angry with my co-worker for treating me unfairly, and I choose to gossip, slander, or seek revenge. I don't feel guilty, so it must not be wrong. When they are fired, the happiness and satisfaction I feel confirms my choices were okay.
- I don't feel close to God, so I guess He must be angry with me or there must be sin in my life.
- I do not experience strong, positive feelings that I am in God's will. Therefore, I can't know what God desires or maybe I am not capable of pleasing Him.
- I am jealous, angry, and resentful of others. Shouldn't I be above that? Why did I let that bother me? I have to hide these "unspiritual" feelings or others will think I am not really a Christian. Maybe I am not saved.
- I don't believe that God has forgiven me or unconditionally loves me because I do not always "feel" forgiven or loveable.

Emotions can be mixed, conflicted, or misunderstood

Various emotions are present at the same time. These mixed emotions can also be in conflict. One who loses their spouse in the line of duty may feel intense anger and loneliness along with deep pride. In an abusive situation, a person can deeply adore the one who harms them while at the same time being absolutely terrified.

Copyright 1998, 2001, 2005, 2007, 2019, 2020 Scope Ministries International, INC.

Emotions can be misdirected

Unmet emotional needs can cause a wide range of feelings. For instance, if we do not perceive acceptance and affection from each parent, our behavior in future relationships can become distorted by substituting physical expressions of intimacy for the missing emotional ones. Feelings of unworthiness or insignificance can drive us to choices that fall very short of those goals. The emotions we experience when depressed, anxious or ashamed will often fuel more negative thoughts which produce deepening feelings of depression, anxiety, and shame. Seeking emotional satisfaction (or avoiding pain) may seem like the only way to feel better but this will not address the message of the emotion or deal with the underlying false beliefs.

Another way our emotions can be misdirected is by displacing them. It is understandable if we are treated badly at work that we hold our tongue to preserve our employment. That can be an exercise in self-control. However, if we hold onto that frustration and anger then dump it on our family when we go home, we will create a mess.

Emotion cannot distinguish between real and imagined events

A perfect example of this is in a movie theater. We know the story on the screen is not real. We know the people we watch are actors and are not living out real life situations as we sit comfortably in a dark room with popcorn and soda. Yet we experience excitement, fear, anger, joy or grief as if we are involved in the scenes because our emotions react the same to reality and fantasy.

The anxiety caused from "What if..." questions can be overwhelming. Anticipating different situations for every thought that pop into our head is not productive planning. These imagined events cause very real stress, excitement and fear without ever taking place.

"If only..." statements can cause strong emotions. Hindsight does give us a broader perspective allowing us to look back on a situation and learn from mistakes. However, continuing to visit the past, feeding grief and regret, or beating ourselves up for not having the foreknowledge to act differently, does not create positive change. It will steer us in circles around past events limiting our ability to move forward.

Other Factors Affect Emotions

Wrong teaching or poor modeling

Our culture has influenced our ability to deal with emotions properly. Children are told not to cry or be angry. Men are often taught not to be

fearful or emotional. Tears are seen as a sign of weakness. Many men and women who have struggled with fear are embarrassed to share this with others and often will not acknowledge their angry feelings to themselves or God.

Physical health

Hormonal changes, stress, fatigue, poor eating, poor sleeping, or lack of exercise can affect us emotionally. In 1 Kings 19, Elijah had seen miraculous displays of God's power and provision on a very personal level. However, he was physically exhausted and became overwhelmed by fear and loneliness. His interpretation of life's circumstances was grossly inaccurate. God met him in the dark moments of this exhaustion and God cared for him with compassion, food and rest knowing Elijah could not care for himself. When thoughts and interpretations are inaccurate, strong feelings can easily follow. Our God is big enough to love us through these strong feelings.

Inversely, emotional health can affect us physically. Anxiety is rampant in our culture. It can cause digestive issues, aggression, tremors and even panic attacks. Emotions affect heart rate, blood pressure and our ability to think clearly. We are spirit, soul and body. Our physical bodies will react to what is found within our soul whether it is turmoil or peace. Praise God that Jesus made peace with us in our spirit!

> *Peace I leave with you; my peace I give you. I do not give to you as the world gives. Do not let your hearts be troubled and do not be afraid.* John 14:27 NIV

Emotions - Stuff or Dump?
One usually leads to the other!

Stuffing

Stepping away from a highly-charged emotional situation in order to let strong emotions lessen in intensity is wise. This is different from "stuffing" which is when we deny or repress our feelings. Denying our feelings and turning them inward is essentially lying to ourselves, God, and others. This can result in physical illness, intense and explosive emotional outbursts, disjointed thoughts and words, or destructive behavior. If we choose to stuff and never allow ourselves to connect these emotions with the appropriate underlying thought they will eventually emerge and will be even harder to address.

Dumping or exploding

Sharing what we feel with trustworthy people is healthy when done in order to receive their help, guidance or to allow ourselves to be known. But all too often we choose to dump our emotions onto others with the

expectation they fix the situation or make us feel better. This can potentially wound them and damage our relationships. We may get our feelings off our chest and feel some temporary relief, but we are not addressing the issues behind the emotions. Some equate "dumping" with healing because of this temporary relief.

Most of us think turning our emotions inward or outward are the only choices we have. Here is some good news, there is another option! We can express our emotions upward.

The Psalms are evidence that David and others felt free to approach God with their emotions. Good examples of how we can do this are found in Psalms 13, 55, and 73.

R.E.E.D.

The acrostic "REED" helps us remember what emotions are for and where to take them. We do not have to be enslaved to our feelings. God desires to help us process our emotions in order to know what message they are sending about our thoughts and beliefs.

Recognize our emotions

We need to acknowledge feelings, not ignore them. We need to learn to verbalize how we feel. Some people have to develop a vocabulary to express how they feel. Sometimes a friend or Biblical Spiritual Advisor can help by giving us objective feedback about the emotions we are experiencing but can't identify. (See a list on page 160.)

Express our emotions to God

Many people are afraid they may offend God if they tell Him how they feel, especially if it is about Him. However, He knows about our feelings and is not offended by them. Our feelings do not change the character of God! When we read the Psalms, we realize that He has heard everything many times before.

God cares about how we feel, and more importantly, why we feel the way we do. When we express our emotions to God, we are being honest with ourselves and with Him. His Spirit and His Word can then direct our thoughts, beliefs, behavior, and eventually, our feelings.

Evaluate what our emotions are telling us

We need to reflect on how our emotions, behavior, and thinking are related. Just as David asked himself, *"Why are you in despair O my soul?"*, we need to ask God to show us what wrong beliefs or thoughts are feeding our emotions.

Copyright 1998, 2001, 2005, 2007, 2019, 2020 Scope Ministries International, INC.

Decide to replace our thinking and behavior with God's Truth

Questions we can ask ourselves: How does what I think and how I behave compare with what God tells me in His Word? What needs to change? Remember we have a new identity and destiny. We do not have to stay stuck in old patterns of living. We can choose to act and react according to our new Biblical thinking. This adjustment of thoughts and beliefs in the light of God's truth is the "renewing of the mind" process that is commanded in Romans 12:2.

> *Do not be conformed any longer to the pattern of this world but be transformed by the renewing of your mind.* Romans 12:2 NIV

Renewing our minds according to God's reality results in our being transformed. As our thinking and beliefs are corrected, our emotions eventually change also.

A word of caution. "REED" is not "four easy steps" to managing your emotions. It is a springboard for interacting actively with God about your deeply felt personal desires and needs. It is important to remember that, as Christians, we are in a vital moment-by-moment relationship with the living God. We often try to define the "Christian life" as a series of principles to be followed rather than total dependence upon, and an active trust in God Himself.

God truly wants to be involved with us in our emotions, in our concerns, in our personal life—more so than our closest friend. He is so much more than a friend, because not only does He empathize, comfort, and advise, but He also transforms us through His Spirit and His Word!

Conclusion

The world around us is clamoring for good feelings while indulging emotions in its search for happiness. Yet, people are not satisfied. They are never quite fulfilled. They are always wanting more. We live by faith rather than feelings, remembering Jesus' words:

> *Blessed and fortunate and happy and spiritually prosperous. . . are those who hunger and thirst for righteousness,. . . for they shall be completely satisfied.* Matthew 5:6 AMPC

One speaker said, "It is normal to have emotions traveling with us in our vehicle, but they shouldn't be allowed to drive. When anything other than our identity in Christ drives our behavior, we have been hijacked!"

If we give control of our actions to feelings, we will be taken to places we do not want to go. We do not deny that our emotions exist, but we do deny that they have authority over us. Only our identity, who we truly are in Christ, is capable and equipped to drive our behavior.

Summary:
1. As God has emotions, we as His creations have emotions.
2. Emotions are messengers to reveal our beliefs.
3. Emotions enable us to enjoy God.
4. Sin has influenced our emotions.
5. Emotions cannot distinguish between real and imagined events.
6. Decide to replace inaccurate beliefs with His Truth.

A Life Transformed, con't.

When I learned that my emotions revealed my false beliefs, the Holy Spirit revealed experiences and situations in my life when I had developed false beliefs about God, myself and others. Although this was painful, it was also a relief to be freed from the lies that I had believed for years. God's truth brought healing.

I learned that emotions are natural because God has created me in His image with emotions like He has. That gave me the freedom to face my emotions for the first time in my life. I always knew that God had emotions like joy and peace, but I was so relieved to learn that He also has emotions like anger. I no longer feel guilty for having emotions like that.

I've learned to recognize the clues when I'm suppressing emotions: drinking coffee, smoking cigarettes, eating when I'm not hungry, cleaning when things aren't dirty, shopping when I don't need anything, writing to-do lists, doing things just to be busy so I don't think. Now when I start to feel like doing one of these things, I talk to God about how I feel and I ask Him, "What is bothering me? Why do I feel this way?" I read the Word to see what He says. After He reveals my wrong beliefs, then I renew my mind with His truth. I say verses out loud when I began to feel like hiding or stuffing my emotions. I often write Scripture verses like Philippians 4:6-7 NIV. *"Don't be anxious about anything, but in everything, by prayer and petition, with thanksgiving, present your requests to God. And the peace of God, which transcends all understanding will guard your hearts and your minds in Christ Jesus."*

I've always known those verses, but now I use them. Instead of trying to handle the problem myself, I turn to God, and He keeps His promise. He does give me His peace!

Over a year ago, I was really hurt by a friend of mine. I tried to contact her by phone and mail, but she didn't respond. I kept turning to God with my emotions when I felt rejected and disliked. I kept trusting Him and praying for her. Recently she sent me a letter asking for forgiveness. If I had continued to let that hurt dominate me, I could have been bitter and unable to give her grace and forgiveness. Instead, our friendship is restored, and God was glorified in it.

I am so grateful I've learned to let my emotions take me to God instead of away from Him. Now I can handle the hurts in my life constructively instead of destructively.

Tammy - Customer Service Representative

Freedom With Emotions - Day 1

Recognize how you deal with negative emotions and begin to interact with God concerning them.

1. What emotions were expressed in your home as you were growing up?

2. Which emotions were "acceptable"? Which ones were "unacceptable"?

3. Presently, what emotions are you comfortable in expressing? Which ones are you comfortable with others expressing?

4. What emotions are you uncomfortable expressing? Which are you uncomfortable with others expressing?

5. What are your "red flags" that indicate you may be feeling an emotion but not acknowledging it? (Examples: yelling, physical stress, short temper, withdrawal, compulsive behavior such as overeating, etc.)

6. Review your answers from Week 1, Day 1. How were your problems affecting you emotionally?

7. Our emotions are messengers alerting us to something in our thoughts and beliefs. What are some thoughts and beliefs that your emotions may reveal?

8. When our emotions are more real to us than God's truth and we base our decisions and responses upon them, then our emotions are messy. Possible responses to these negative emotions include denying, "stuffing," venting on others, and expressing them to God. How have you handled these negative emotions in the past? (Example: When I feel depressed, I ignore it by eating or watching TV.)

9. How did these emotions affect your behavior and/or choices?

10. Take a few moments to interact with God. First, compare your beliefs, thoughts, and behaviors with God's Word. Ask the Holy Spirit to reveal to you any inconsistencies and confess (agree with God) those that He reveals. Then, decide how you need to change your thoughts, beliefs, and behavior to be consistent with God's truth. Next, ask the Holy Spirit to help change your behavior and to continue to reveal incorrect beliefs and thoughts. Remember, each time you experience a negative emotion or the Holy Spirit reveals a wrong belief or thought, it can be replaced with God's truth.

Freedom With Emotions - Day 2

Recognize the emotional side of God in Scripture.

1. Read the following verses, and list the emotions that God expresses.

Genesis 6:5-6

Psalm 145:8

Psalm 149:4

Isaiah 57:16

Isaiah 62:5

Mark 10:21

Luke 13:34

Luke 22:44

John 11:33-36

Hebrews 5:7

2. Compare and/or contrast these verses with how you have previously viewed God.

3. Read the following verses to learn how God feels about your emotions. Write how God feels about or responds to your emotions.

Psalm 51:17

Psalm 56:8

Matthew 11:28

John 20:24-28

Hebrews 4:15-16

1 Peter 5:7

4. Compare and/or contrast these verses with how you have previously thought God feels about your emotions.

Freedom With Emotions - Day 3

See a Biblical pattern for processing your emotions.

1. The Biblical pattern for REED (what to do with emotions) is especially noticeable in Psalms 55 and 73.
    Recognize your emotions.
    Express them to God (don't ignore them, stuff them or lash out toward others).
    Evaluate what your emotions and thoughts reveal about what you are believing
       (ask the Holy Spirit to show you).
    Decide to agree with God about the truth (believe), and act in faith on that truth.

REED applies to both positive and negative emotions. Even negative emotions can be helpful as we turn to God and evaluate our thinking and beliefs.

2. Read Psalm 73 in the chronological order provided below and answer the questions.

RECOGNIZE: (verses 2-14) What emotions does the Psalmist experience?

EXPRESS: (verses 16, 21-22) How does the Psalmist express his emotions to God? List some of the statements he makes.

EVALUATE: (verses 17-20, 1, 23-27) What beliefs do his emotions reveal?

DECIDE: (verse 28) How does the Psalmist choose to act on the truth (rather than on his emotions)?

3. Ask the Holy Spirit to remind you to practice REED in your communication with God.

Freedom With Emotions - Day 4

Practice using the REED method.

1. Emotions, both pleasant and unpleasant, are a normal part of the Christian life.
    Think back to the last time you were struggling with negative emotions. Use the chart on page 160 to help you recognize your feelings and list them below.

2. Now express your feelings to God by writing the thoughts that prompted you to feel this way. Be as honest as possible. God already knows and accepts you. He never condemns or rejects you because of your emotional struggles.

3. Emotions are the result of thoughts and beliefs. Now, evaluate your thoughts by answering the following questions:

    A. What beliefs do your thoughts reveal about God, yourself, and your circumstances?

    B. What is the truth according to God's Word? (Refer to the Lesson The **Truth About Your New Identity** (page 85 for the truth).

4. Next, decide to reject the lies you've been thinking and to replace them with the truth. Make a deliberate choice to walk by faith, accepting God's Word as your final authority. Ask God what steps of faith (action) He wants you to take.

5. For the rest of this week practice the REED method whenever you encounter negative or painful emotions. You may want to journal (write) your thoughts and feelings.

Freedom With Emotions - Day 5

Recognize and express your fears to God and learn to trust in Him when you are afraid.

One of our most painful emotions is fear—which is often disguised as worry, anger, or depression. It is one of the most difficult emotions to acknowledge. We have been taught that fear is a sign of weakness; therefore, we've learned to suppress it.

1. King David, a man after God's heart, often experienced fear. Read Psalm 56.

2. What did David fear? (see verses 2, 5-6)

3. What did David do when he was afraid? (see verses 1, 3-4, 9-13)

4. Think of a specific situation which causes you to be afraid. It might be a future event, or it may be the fear of failure or rejection. Use the REED method for taking this fear to God.

RECOGNIZE: Ask God to help you identify what you are afraid of. Acknowledge your fear to yourself and God.

EXPRESS: Write to God what you fear and why you are afraid.

EVALUATE: Consider what your thoughts and feelings tell you about your beliefs about this issue. What beliefs about God does your fear reveal? How does what you think and believe compare with God's Word?

DECIDE: Choose to agree with God's truth about this issue. Then, choose to act on that truth, knowing that the Holy Spirit will empower you.

Example: "Father, I am afraid my husband may lose his job. It's hard for me to trust You in this area when I think of our family's needs. Thank You for listening and caring about how I feel. I know You promise to meet all our needs (Philippians 4:19), so I am casting all my cares on You (1 Peter 5:7). Therefore, I choose to go about my day, not focusing on the potential problem, but trusting You to work this out for our good and to meet our needs in Your way and in Your timing."

Freedom With Emotions - Lesson Six Summary

Name _____ Date _____

Answer the following questions.

1. What negative emotion did you experience most this past week? What kind of thoughts usually produced this emotion?

2. What did these thoughts tell you about what you were believing?

3. What new insight or perspective did God give you when you expressed your feelings honestly to Him?

4. How will practicing REED improve your relationship with God and your quality of life?

5. Mark the graph to indicate how much of this week's assignment you completed.

0%_____50%_____100%

How Do You Feel?

Lonely			Belonging		
left out	isolated	separate	popular	important	influential
friendless	withdrawn	rejected	famous	well-known	valuable
forsaken	lonesome		needed	accepted	worthwhile
lost	insignificant			attached	

Angry			Peaceful		
furious	mad	frustrated	calm	collected	composed
hacked off	hard	boiling	quiet	sedate	cool
aggravated	irritated	indignant	serene	content	tranquil
	distant	annoyed			

Sad			Happy		
dejected	depressed	gloomy	joyful	glad	bright
unhappy	cheerless	glum	ecstatic	pleased	vivacious
dreary	blue	downcast	cheerful	delighted	elated
woeful	grieving	heavy	upbeat	light	bouncy

Afraid			Secure		
anxious	fearful	scared	safe	optimistic	hopeful
frightened	shocked	terrified	protected	sure	confident
alarmed	unnerved	timid	stable	poised	assured
jumpy	tight	shaky			

Hateful			Loving		
hostile	critical	jealous	tender	accepting	loyal
unfriendly	quarrelsome	spiteful	affectionate	kind	sympathetic
mean	nasty	harsh	warm	devoted	caring
	shameful			forgiving	

Inadequate			Powerful		
weak	bashful	inept	strong	great	sure
small	meager	powerless	energetic	dominant	aggressive
useless	deficient	vulnerable	assertive	pushy	confident
			upbeat	assured	intoxicated

Guilty			Innocent		
ashamed	damned	judged	pardoned	set free	naive
criticized	doomed	trapped	pure	released	acquitted
cursed	dirty	embarrassed	forgiven	exonerated	justified
			clean	fresh	

page 160   Copyright 1998, 2001, 2005, 2007, 2019, 2020   Scope Ministries International, INC.

FORGIVENESS = freedom

Freedom in Forgiveness

"And be kind to one another, tender-hearted, forgiving each other, just as God in Christ also has forgiven you."
Ephesians 4:32 NASB

Lesson Seven

A Life Transformed

In April 1995 my life appeared to be great. I was married to a wonderful man, and we had two precious children. We were financially stable. I had many friends. My career was progressing. We attended a friendly church. But underneath the smile was a pain so deep that depression had nearly overtaken me. I felt as though I had fallen into a deep, dark hole. The harder I tried to climb out, the deeper I sank. At times, just getting up each morning was nearly impossible. At work I would sit at my desk and stare at my computer for hours. Even at home, I was so depressed that all I wanted to do was sleep. My facade of happiness covered an emotional pain that was deeply rooted in my childhood. I was the youngest of six children. My parents were successful people who were extremely active in church. On the surface, my family life appeared normal, but the "game" my brother, seven years older, played with me was far from normal. From the time I was five until I was 11 years old, my older brother frequently asked me to go to the game room above our garage where he sexually abused me.

I knew that at least part of the reason for my depression was the abuse. I had lived with flashbacks and pain for many years with memories haunting me daily. I thought that I deserved this because I blamed myself for the abuse, and I thought it was my fault that it had lasted so long. I knew that I couldn't continue my life this way and that I had to be free from depression.

I contacted Scope Ministries and asked for help. I confided my struggles to a sweet lady who, week after week, lovingly responded to my pain with Scriptures. The Word of God started seeping into my spirit to begin healing me. During the next six months, I talked with her weekly, I read scores of books, I listened to many tapes, and I memorized many scriptures. I'll never forget the day that I realized that the abuse was not my fault.

At this point, one of my greatest fears was confronting my brother. We both had spent many years pretending that the abuse never happened. After six months of dealing with this agonizing issue, I felt that I needed to confront him and face the painful results of the abuse in my life. I was ready for confrontation and forgiveness and healing.

I needed to confront my brother because, even with the memories, I still had some doubt that the abuse had really occurred. By acknowledging it, I removed all my doubts that it really happened. It was one of the toughest things I've ever done, but I wrote him a letter and then waited to see if and how he would respond. Would he deny it? Trivialize it? Blame me? I really just didn't know.

to be continued...

Freedom in Forgiveness — Lesson Seven

Back in lesson 3 you were introduced to three-part man (body, soul, and spirit). These three parts are three types of life – body life (*Bios* in Greek), soul life (*Psuche* in Greek), and spirit life (*Zoe* in Greek). In the English language, biology comes from the word *Bios* and psychology from the word *Psuche*. In lesson 2 you learned that because of sin you were dead in the spirit (Colossians 2:13-14). Obviously, you were not dead physically (body) or in your soul (mind, will, and emotions). The only avenue for life in an unbeliever is body life or soul life because they are dead to God in the spirit. Without Zoe life to meet the deepest longings of our hearts we go looking for life in other areas (i.e. body and soul). So how do we seek life from the body or soul?

Through the body we seek life through beauty, sports, physical abilities, or our sexuality. Through the soul we seek life through the intellect, attention, praise, personality, will-power, success, or relationships. If we exclusively depend on these areas for a sense of life, acceptance, excitement, and purpose, we will eventually be disappointed. Why? Those areas were never intended to meet the deepest longings of our heart. For example, if we spend hours on beautifying ourselves to gain attention, what happens when others fail to praise us or notice us? We get angry. Why? We experience anger when our beauty fails to make us feel accepted, noticed, or praised.

Expectations and Anger

As we saw in the previous lesson, our "unpleasant" emotions can be an obstacle in believing God's truth. One "unpleasant" emotion is anger. Anger is one of the strongest of emotions yet itself is not sinful, *"be angry, and yet do not sin"* (Ephesians 4:26). Both God (Holy), and Jesus (without sin) expressed the emotion of anger. Anger can be likened to power, sex, or fire. These things are neither inherently right nor wrong, but they become right or wrong only as they are used properly or abused. To determine if anger is appropriate, we can identify the basis and expression of our anger. Unmet expectations are not the only cause of anger.

The Webster's New World College Dictionary Fourth Edition 1999 defines anger as "a feeling of displeasure resulting from injustice, injury, mistreatment, opposition, etc., and usually showing itself in a desire to fight back at the supposed cause of this feeling; intense displeasure or exasperation; an emotional state of hostility, indignation, and revenge." In a real sense anger is just an indicator (like a dashboard light in the car) revealing that we have been injured either intentionally or unintentionally. You choose how you respond to anger. You can choose to ignore the warning light on the dashboard to the peril of your car.

The Apostle Peter, at the time of Jesus' arrest, is a good example of an inappropriate response caused by the emotion of anger.

> *"And behold, one of those who were with Jesus reached and drew out his sword, and struck the slave of the high priest, and cut off his ear. Then Jesus said to him, "Put your sword back into its place; for all those who take up the sword shall perish by the sword."* Matthew 26:51-54, NASB

Peter's anger was based on his love for Christ, but he failed to control the expression of his anger. Anger was not the problem, but the expression of his anger was inappropriate.

How Can We Prevent Inappropriate Expressions of Anger?

First, **yield your expectations and rights to God**. In yielding, choose to let God meet your needs in the ways He sees best instead of the way you want to get your needs met. Choose to trust and look to Him as the source of your contentment instead of looking to circumstances and people to give joy and meet your needs.

Second, **acknowledge your anger to yourself and God**. Own it. To respond to anger you need to identify anger. Anger becomes a problem when we respond to it improperly.

Third, **ask God to reveal the source of your anger** – Why am I angry? Why was I offended? What was I owed – respect, love etc.? What was the offense, unmet expectation, or blocked goal? What did I expect? How did I want them to respond? What did I really need?

Fourth, **express your anger to God**. It is vital that we express our anger to God and allow Him to show us the cause of our anger. If we choose to ignore or suppress our anger, it will manifest itself in our behavior, eventually affecting our emotional and/or physical health.

Finally, **ask Christ to reveal His love and grace to the offender through you.**

Why is it Important to Confront our Anger?

Anger leads to bitterness

When we don't address our anger properly, we will develop a root of bitterness. The Biblical definition of bitterness is "resentfulness" or "harshness" and is referred to specifically in Ephesians 4:31 and Hebrews 12:15.

> *"Let all bitterness and wrath and anger and clamor and slander be put away from you, along with all malice."*

Ephesians 4:31 NASB
See to it that no one comes short of the grace of God; that no root of bitterness springing up causes trouble, and by it many be defiled.
Hebrews 12:15 NASB

Bitterness is the result of a perceived right that has been violated. Bitterness develops from unforgiveness and unacknowledged anger over a long period of time.

Unforgiveness tries to hold the offender responsible (guilty) for his wrong. The mind will begin to accumulate evidence to show fault. When the opportunity arises, we dump our case on the offender. When we choose unforgiveness, we secretly await the "joy" of seeing the offender punished by God. This is a form of vengeance.

Ultimately unforgiveness gives our abuser permission to continue to abuse us. How? We think about them, going over the offense endlessly, and have conversations in our mind ("then I'd say…. and tell him how mean he was, etc.")

Bitterness causes emotional, physical and spiritual bondage

When we are bitter towards a person, we may think we are hurting that person, but really we are hurting ourselves. Bitterness creates a feeling of distance in our fellowship with God. Emotionally, it can cause anxiety, stress, and depression. Physically, it can cause symptons from headaches and fatigue to ulcers and arthritis. Unresolved anger also gives Satan an opportunity to wreak havoc in our lives.

> *". . do not let the sun go down on your anger, and do not give the devil an opportunity."* Ephesians 4:26b-27 NASB

Bitterness affects not only us but will contaminate all our relationships. Hebrews 12:15

Bitterness is like a cancer. Just as cancer will eventually spread throughout our entire body, bitterness will eventually affect all our relationships. A bitter person becomes critical, cynical, hateful, and harsh.

In His love, God desires to free us from this renegade emotion. His solution is forgiveness. He clearly instructs us to love our enemies and do good to those who mistreat us (Luke 6:27-28).

> *And be kind to one another, tender-hearted, forgiving each other, just as God in Christ also has forgiven you.* Ephesians 4:32 NAS

Forgiveness Frees Us

We choose to forgive those who have blocked our goals, injured us or not fulfilled our expectations. If we do not deal with the bitterness, its roots grow into resentment, vengeance, and depression. We will become unable to be satisfied, and we will focus totally on our unmet expectations and the ones who failed to meet them. This blinds us as to how God is meeting our needs.

Forgiveness is a characteristic of our new identity in Christ. Since we have Christ's forgiving life in us we have the ability to forgive. Unforgiveness in our lives will make us miserable because we deny His forgiving life within us. It is in our nature as God's children to forgive others as God has forgiven us.

God forgiving you motivates and allows you to forgive others.

> . . . *bearing with one another, and forgiving each other, whoever has a complaint against anyone; just as the Lord forgave you, so also should you.*
> Colossians 3:13, NASB

Forgiveness is more than an outward behavior. Forgiveness is a life – His life which dwells in His children.

Forgiveness is not ignoring, disregarding, tolerating, excusing, overlooking or closing our eyes to the wrong another person has done against us. It is not simply letting time pass after the offense has been committed. It is not trying to forget that the offense happened or pretending that it didn't. It is not just resigning ourselves to the other person's actions by saying, "Well, that's just the way he is."

Forgiveness is not putting ourselves in the position to be abused or victimized again.

Forgiveness is a deliberate decision to cancel the debt owed. Before you can cancel a debt you have to "charge" or specify the debt. In order for a credit card company to forgive a debt there has to be a debt (charges).

Forgiveness is foregoing what we feel is due us and declaring the person no longer guilty toward us. It involves relinquishing the right to punish or to get even. It is relinquishing the right to judge or condemn the person for what they have done. Forgiveness is giving up the demand that they make right the wrong done.

The process of forgiveness includes:

1. Acknowledging the offense to God.
2. Expressing to God how it made you feel.
3. Expressing to God your decision to cancel the debt.
   - Giving up the right to punish or get even.
   - Giving up the right to judge or condemn.
   - Giving up the demand that they make right the wrong done.
4. Accepting the person just as they are.
   - Yield expectations to God.
   - Trust God to meet your needs.
   - Pray God's best for that individual.
5. Being willing to risk being hurt again - in a normal relational sense. (We are not saying you should let your self be abused and victimized phyically and sexually!)
   - Take down any walls of self-protection.
   - Trust God to heal and protect you should you be hurt again.

Forgiveness requires our trust in God's character. We trust in God's faithfulness to work everything out for good, even in our injury and pain.

Forgiveness is not:

ignoring/disregarding the wrong done

tolerating the person

excusing the person

forgetting about the wrong done

letting time pass

allowing abuse (boundaries should be set)

being nice to the person

keeping silent

saying, "I forgive you."

based on feelings

Forgiveness is:

canceling a debt owed

giving the person to God

yielding our rights to God

trusting God to redeem the situation

Copyright 1998, 2001, 2005, 2007, 2019, 2020 Scope Ministries International, INC..

yielding our right to punish

not seeking revenge or getting even

not judging or condemning

not keeping score

extending mercy and grace

making a conscious choice

And as for you, you meant evil against me, but God meant it for good . . .
Genesis 50:20a, NASB

And we know that God causes all things to work together for good to those who love God, to those who are called according to His purpose.
Romans 8:28, NASB

Even after we have made the choice to forgive, the emotions of anger and bitterness may still linger. Our emotions will eventually reflect God's heart of grace, mercy and compassion as we continue to renew our minds with truth and reaffirm our decision to forgive.

What if our bitterness is toward God?

Even when we are angry at God, He does not condemn or become angry with us. He is committed to us and always responds with grace, mercy and love. Therefore, when we are angry with God, we need to choose to trust in God's graceful, loving and merciful character. We choose to trust that He is working all the circumstances in our life for our good (Romans 8:28) and that He will provide for our every need (Philippians 4:19). We need to honestly express our anger to Him and allow Him to reveal wrong beliefs we have about Him. There are many examples of this in Scripture. David, a man after God's own heart, freely expressed his anger toward God in Psalm 13:1-6 NASB.

How long, O Lord? Wilt Thou forget me forever?

How long wilt Thou hide Thy face from me?

How long shall I take counsel in my soul,

Having sorrow in my heart all the day?

How long will my enemy be exalted over me?

After expressing His anger, David chose to trust in God's character.

But I have trusted in Thy lovingkindness;

My heart shall rejoice in Thy salvation.

I will sing to the Lord,

Because He has dealt bountifully with me.

Forgiving others has many benefits in our life including sensing a heavy burden or weight taken off our shoulders. God desires that forgiveness become a part of our lifestyle. Unforgiveness is a burden we were not created to bear. A few of the personal benefits that are often experienced through forgiveness are:

- Emotional healing;
- Healthier relationships;
- Increased intimacy with God;
- Physical healing; and
- Freedom from spiritual oppression

Conclusion:

We have examined how expectations lead to anger which can lead to bitterness. These need to be recognized and acknowledged to God. As we interact with our Heavenly Father, He will reveal to us the cause(s) so we can trust Him with His solution. Anger is common to all. Christ has truly set us free from being controlled by expectations, anger and bitterness. As we walk in the Spirit, His love and forgiveness will be the controlling factor in our lives. As His children we are now free to forgive finding **Freedom in Forgiveness**!

Summary:
1. Anger can result from blocked goals or unmet expectations. Unresolved anger leads to bitterness. Part of God's solution is to yield our expectations and rights to Him. God's solution is looking to His (Zoe) life within to meet our deepest needs.

2. Bitterness can result from a perceived right or expectation that has been violated. God's solution for bitterness begins with understanding and receiving God's complete forgiveness.

3. By receiving God's forgiveness we can make a deliberate choice to forgive others.

Forgiveness is primarily for our benefit.

A Life Transformed, con't.

To my relief, he wrote me, admitting the abuse. He said that I would probably never be able to forgive him, but that he wished that somehow I could.

Because my brother lives out-of-state, I didn't expect to see him for a while, but just a week after I received his letter, my father passed away unexpectedly. I knew that he would be in town for the funeral, and I was uneasy because I didn't know what to expect. He asked me to talk, and when we got together, I felt for the first time that I could truly forgive. It wasn't a forgiveness that I was mustering within myself but a forgiveness that only the Holy Spirit could produce within me. I knew because Christ forgave me when I didn't deserve it, I could forgive my brother even though he didn't deserve it.

When I told my brother that I forgave him for the abuse, he broke into tears. I was crying too as I hugged him. I knew that I needed to forgive him even more than he needed me to forgive him. At that precise moment, a heavy weight lifted from my shoulders. All the years of painful memories were washed away.

Many things have changed in my life since that moment. Through forgiveness, I let go of the bitterness that I had carried for so many years. Now I no longer experience flashbacks, and when I do remember the abuse, it is without the pain that used to engulf me. As I let go of my anger, God replaced my depression with His peace. Now my everyday struggles don't overwhelm me like before.

Now I am better able to express my love to my family. Instead of assuming that my husband and children know that I love them, I try to tell them more often. It's been difficult because I was never taught to say those three little words, "I love you," but it's been rewarding.

I am so grateful to the Lord for healing my emotions. I can't explain how different I feel each day when I wake up. It is such a sweet release to be at peace.

Marge - Writer/Editor

Freedom in Forgiveness - Day One

Goal: To gain a Biblical perspective of anger and recognize the underlying cause of it.

When you acknowledge and take responsibility for your anger, victory over the anger becomes a distinct probability rather than a remote possibility. You may have "reason" for your anger, but do you have the "right" to stay angry? Have you reserved for yourself the "right" to be angry? No matter the reason for your anger, understand that you CHOOSE to stay angry.

1. To gain a Biblical perspective of anger, write out the main point of the following passages.

Proverbs 29:11

Proverbs 19:11

Proverbs 29:22

Ephesians 4:26-27

Colossians 3:8-9

James 1:19-20

2. List at least five expectations you have of yourself or others which, when not met, make you feel angry (irritated, frustrated, outraged, etc.). Circle the "+" if you think these expectations are presently being met, and circle the "-" if you think they are not being met.

a) _____ + -

b) _____ + -

c) _____ + -

d) _____ + -

e) _____ + -

3. Everyone has needs. When our needs are not met, we often feel hurt or angry. Listed below are needs that we have. Circle the "+" if you think the need is being met, and circle the "-" if you think the need is not being met. Circle the letter that corresponds with the person(s) you think should meet this need: (Y) Yourself, (S) Spouse, (P) Parent, (O) Others.

1) To be loved   Y S   P O   +   -
2) To be needed   Y S   P O   +   -
3) To be understood   Y S   P O   +   -
4) To be wanted   Y S   P O   +   -
5) To be cared for   Y S   P O   +   -
6) To have significance   Y S   P O   +   -
7) To be approved of   Y S   P O   +   -
8) To be secure   Y S   P O   +   -
9) To belong   Y S   P O   +   -
10) To be fulfilled   Y S   P O   +   -

4. One of the major causes of anger is thinking that our "rights" have been denied. Which of the "rights" listed below do you think of as being your personal "right"? Circle the "-" if the right is being denied, and list by whom the right is being denied.

                                                            By Whom

1) To be treated fairly   -   _____
2) To make my own decisions   -   _____
3) To date   -   _____
4) To have self-expression   -   _____
5) To do my own thing   -   _____
6) To be obeyed   -   _____
7) To have my own money   -   _____
8) To have privacy   -   _____
9) To have my own opinion   -   _____
10) To have my own friends   -   _____
11) To be protected   -   _____
12) To be free   -   _____
13) To be appreciated   -   _____
14) To be heard   -   _____
15) To receive affection   -   _____

5. Read Philippians 2:5-11. What rights do you think Jesus surrendered? Are you willing to yield your rights and trust God to meet your needs and exalt you in His way and in His time? As you pray about this, ask God to empower you to surrender your rights to Him.

Freedom in Forgiveness - Day Two

Goal: To learn to prevent and deal with anger by recognizing and yielding expectations to God.

When an expectation is blocked or unmet, our immediate emotional response is anger. Ephesians 4:26-27 reads, *"be angry, and yet do not sin; do not let the sun go down on your anger, and do not give the devil an opportunity (*foothold)." Unresolved anger leads to bitterness, and bitterness to resentment, vengeance, ingratitude, and depression.

1. Read over the "Freedom in Forgiveness Worksheet"

    Describe a situation that causes you continual anger.

2. What expectations are unmet? If you don't know, refer to Day One answers.

3. Choose to yield your expectations to God, and trust Him to meet your need in whatever way HE sees best. How would this change your response to the situation or person?

Anger as an emotion is not sinful. Wrong beliefs, attitudes, and actions which result from unresolved anger are what can be sinful and need to be changed.

And do not grieve the Holy Spirit of God, by whom you were sealed for the day of redemption. Let all bitterness and wrath and anger and clamor and slander be put away from you, along with all malice. And be kind to one another, tender-hearted, forgiving each other, just as God in Christ also has forgiven you. Ephesians 4:30-32 NAS

4. Which of your beliefs, attitudes, or actions need to change? Whom do you need to forgive?

5. Write a prayer asking God to enable you to forgive and to accept those who are not fulfilling your expectations (whether or not those expectations are founded).

Freedom in Forgiveness - Day Three

Goal: To understand God's forgiveness and recognize obstacles to forgiving yourself and others.

1. Often we have misconceptions about forgiveness. Read the list of "Common Misconceptions Regarding Forgiveness" on page 184, and check those misconceptions you have held about forgiveness.

2. Unforgiveness is difficult especially when we have received God's total forgiveness. Is there anything that you have done, thought, or felt that still causes you to feel shame or guilt?

3. Read Matthew 18:21-35. Jesus taught this parable to demonstrate four important aspects of forgiveness:

    1) Forgiveness is a gift we do not deserve.

    2) It is erasing or foregoing what we feel is due us, canceling the debt owed, and yielding our rights and expectations.

    3) Once received from God, it is to be given to others.

    4) Unforgiveness results in personal torture and inner torment.

4. In Christ there is complete forgiveness.

    And when you were dead in your transgressions and the uncircumcision of your flesh, He made you alive together with Him, having forgiven us ALL our transgressions, having canceled out the certificate of debt consisting of decrees against us and which was hostile to us; and He has taken it out of the way, and nailed it to the cross. Colossians 2:13-14, NAS (emphasis added)

In the Roman courts of law, when a person was charged with a crime, a "certificate of debt" was written against him. This indictment stated the charge or charges against the person, and a due penalty was demanded. If the person charged was found guilty, he was taken to prison. The "certificate of debt" was nailed to his prison door. Once he had completed his sentence he was freed, and the words "paid in full" were stamped on the certificate of debt. The last words of Jesus on the cross were "It is finished." Incredibly, the word "finished" is the same word that was stamped on the certificate of debt, "paid in full"! Jesus paid in full the penalty for all our sins.

> *By this will we have been sanctified through the offering of the body of Jesus Christ once for all. And every priest stands daily ministering and offering time after time the same sacrifices, which can never take away sins; but He, having offered one sacrifice for sins for all time, SAT DOWN AT THE RIGHT HAND OF GOD, . . . For by one offering He has perfected for all time those who are sanctified. "AND THEIR SINS AND THEIR LAWLESS DEEDS I WILL REMEMBER NO MORE." Now where there is forgiveness of these things, there is no longer any offering for sin. Since, therefore, brethren, we have confidence to enter the holy place by the blood of Jesus.* Hebrews 10:10-12, 14, 17-19 NAS (emphasis added)

Is there any sin that Jesus hasn't forgiven? What?

5. It is essential and imperative that you accept what God has accomplished through His blood sacrifice on the Cross and receive His total and complete forgiveness. Verbalize your gratitude to Him (be specific).

Freedom in Forgiveness - Day Four

Goal: To begin resolving any unforgiveness and bitterness in your life.

Forgiveness is a decision, a choice based on an act of the will, not a feeling. It is a rational choice I make because I have been totally and completely forgiven by God. I have been made a forgiving person by nature in Christ. Therefore, not to forgive is to act contrary to my identity in Christ. Therefore, forgiveness includes:

a. Acknowledging the hurt.

b. Acknowledging how I felt.

c. Releasing the person from the debt owed me. (Saying in effect: "You never have to make it up to me or repay me. You are now free. You are forgiven. I release you...the debt is canceled.")

d. Accepting the person unconditionally, just as he is, and letting God change him. It requires releasing the person from the responsibility to love and accept me. I look to Christ alone to meet my need for security and significance and yield the right to judge the other person.

e. Being willing to risk being hurt again in the future should God allow it. In other words, I take down my wall of self-protection and trust Christ as my Wisdom and Protection should I get hurt again.

1. Some reasons why we fail to forgive are listed on page 187. Circle the number of each one that applies to you.

2. Describe an incident in your past that causes ongoing hurt.

3. On a separate piece of paper list each person who has contributed to your hurt, specifically stating the offense and the resulting emotions. The following outline may be helpful.

1) "God, it hurt me when . . . " (Be specific).

2) "And I felt . . . "

3) "I now choose to forgive _____. "

4) "I accept _____ unconditionally, which means my love and acceptance of _____ does not depend on _____ or _____ performance now or in the future. I accept _ just the way _____ is . . . even if _____ never changes…even if _____._____ gets worse."

5) "I release _____ from the responsibility to meet my needs for love and acceptance. I choose to trust Jesus alone as the only one who can truly meet all my needs."

6) "I am willing to risk being hurt again by _____ and trust Jesus as my Wisdom and Protection in the future about _____ and this matter."

7) "God, I give You permission to change or to not change my feelings, according to Your time schedule."

Remember, forgiveness is primarily for your benefit. Revealing to the offender that you have forgiven is not necessary or desirable unless he requests your forgiveness.

4. Now after you have walked through the steps of forgiveness, destroy this list.

Freedom in Forgiveness - Day Five

Goal: To recognize and remove a root of bitterness.

Bitterness is to the soul what cholesterol is to the arteries. Bitterness blocks the flow of the living water, limiting our ability to be filled with the Holy Spirit.

> *And do not grieve the Holy Spirit of God, by whom you were sealed for the day of redemption. Let all bitterness and wrath and anger and clamor and slander be put away from you, along with all malice.* Ephesians 4:30-31 NAS

> *Pursue peace with all men . . . See to it that no one comes short of the grace of God; that no root of bitterness springing up causes trouble, and by it many be defiled.* Hebrews 12:14a, 15 NASB

The root of bitterness is invisible, but it produces visible fruit such as:

- Withdrawal from God
- Inability to love others
- Spiritual doubt and unbelief
- Depression
- Physical problems

The solution for bitterness is forgiveness. Cleansing our hearts of bitterness is often a long process when there has been an accumulation of unresolved anger and hurt. The following exercise may take some extra time to complete. No matter how long it takes, it will be worth it. Gaining freedom from bitterness will bring new freedom and joy in your life.

1. Ask the Holy Spirit to bring to your mind each event in your past that still stands out as an unpleasant or painful experience. Make a list on a separate piece of paper, writing down just a few words to identify the incident.

2. Below each incident list each person who contributed to your hurt.

3. List each wrong you suffered from each person.

4. Review the handout, "Reasons Why I Don't Forgive" on page 187. Note which ones apply in each situation.

Remember, forgiveness is primarily for your benefit. Now it is your nature to forgive as God has forgiven you.

5. One by one, verbalize to God your decision to forgive each person. Yield your "right" to punish the person in any way. Trust God to deal with each one as He sees best (Romans 12:19). *

6. Thank God for His faithfulness to use even the most hurtful incidents in your life for your ultimate good (Genesis 50:20; 1 Thessalonians 5:18; Romans 8:28).

7. Ask God to help you see each person who has hurt you the way He does and to empower you to love each one unconditionally (Matthew 5:43-48; Luke 6:27-38).

8. When you have completed this exercise, write "Paid In Full" across your list, and destroy it,

* If you still find this too painful or difficult, you may need a trusted friend, pastor, or Biblical personal guidance minister to pray with you.

Freedom in Forgiveness - Lesson Seven Summary

Name_____Date _____

Answer the following questions. To turn in this page to small group leader..

1. About which event have you been the most angry?

2. What expectations or rights are you holding onto that are contributing to this anger?

3. How are unforgiveness and bitterness affecting your life and relationships?

4. Have you forgiven those who have hurt you? If not, what do you think are the obstacles to forgiving them?

5. Whom did God lead you to forgive through this assignment?

6. Mark the graph to indicate how much of this week's assignment you completed.

None_____50%_____100%

Record Your Prayer Requests:

Freedom in Forgiveness Worksheet

Throughout life, we all develop expectations. They are usually produced by comparing ourselves with others ("They get to, so why can't I?") or from commitments people make or imply. Some expectations result from valid needs in our lives, such as being loved, accepted, and feeling secure. We naturally expect (perhaps demand) others to meet our needs or wants. When those expectations are not met in the ways we want them to be met by others or by God, the emotional reaction is often anger.

The Bible says to "be angry, and yet do not sin" (Ephesians 4:26). Anger becomes a problem when we deal with it improperly. A way to safeguard against responding in anger is to yield our expectations to God. In yielding, I choose to let God meet my needs in the ways He sees best, not in the ways in which I want to see things done. I decide to trust Him and look to Him as the source of my contentment, joy, and security, instead of looking to circumstances or to other people.

However, what if I don't recognize an expectation I have and I get angry? What if the anger remains in my heart and turns into bitterness? To deal with anger and bitterness, I can choose to forgive others for what has happened and release them from my expectations. God will deal with them, so I defer that right to Him. If I do not deal with the bitterness, its roots spiral down into resentment, vengeance, and depression (Hebrews 12:15). I become unable to be satisfied and focus totally on the unmet expectation and the one who failed to meet it. I become unable to see how God is meeting my needs. But, what if the anger is at God? Then, I must make a choice to trust in God's loving and merciful character, that He is working all circumstances in my life for the good (Romans 8:28) and that He will provide my every need (Philippians 4:19) in His way.

Assignment

1. List any incident in your past that causes ongoing hurt. List each person who has contributed to your hurts.

2. Ask God to make you willing to forgive these people, and even yourself, and to trust Him to work all together for good.

3. By faith, choose to forgive the offenders by an act of your will, apart from what your emotions or reason are telling you. Verbalize this choice to God. Trust God to change your feelings of anger and hurt in His timing.

COMMON MISCONCEPTIONS REGARDING FORGIVENESS

I feel like I have forgiven _____ because: (check those that apply)

_____I don't feel angry anymore. Forgiveness is not feeling angry anymore.

_____I am able to justify, understand, and explain away this person's hurtful behavior. I can see some of the reasons why he did it.

_____I am able to put myself in his shoes and see things from his point of view.

_____I am able to separate the person from their behavior. Forgiveness is being able to say, "What a person does and who he is, are two different things."

_____I am giving him the benefit of the doubt. He didn't mean it. Forgiveness says no one is perfect, so you need to cut people some slack.

_____I am saying to myself "time heals all wounds." I am willing to be patient and go on with my life.

_____Forgiveness is a process that takes a lot of time.

_____I am willing just to forget about it. Forgiving is forgetting…it is saying, "Let's just forget about it."

_____I am able to pray for the person who has hurt me. I have asked God to forgive him.

_____I am waiting for him to come to me and ask for my forgiveness. Once he does this, I will forgive him. I am willing to forgive.

_____I have confronted this person about his behavior.

_____I am able to say that I haven't really been hurt that badly. I just pretend that the hurt was really not that big of a thing.

_____I am able to act as if it never happened.

_____I have attempted reconciliation. Forgiveness says that the broken relationship must be restored.

_____I am willing to go to the person and tell him that I forgive him.

_____I am willing to be nice, take him a gift, and "turn the other cheek."

_____I am trying to behave in a forgiving manner.

_____I am trying to pretend that everything is OK and go on with my life and not bring the matter up again.

In short, forgiveness is none of the above items. Some of these may help in the process of getting ready to forgive, or they may be products of the forgiveness process, but they are not actually the same as forgiveness.

Reasons I Don't Forgive

(the reason is in regular type, the truth is in *italics*)

1. Pride: forgiving someone makes me look weak. I want to be strong and superior. I'm right and I don't have to give in. *But pride is what keeps me in bondage and hinders growth.*

2. I don't want to give up my excuse-making system. *At first, freedom can be scary. I am out of my comfort zone. I will be learning a whole new way of living if I learn to forgive.*

3. If I were to forgive I would feel out of control. I want to feel in control and be able to manipulate others by holding the debt against them. *The truth is I am out of control when I cling to my hurt. I am the one in bondage.*

4. If I forgive, I may get hurt again. *The truth is I am going to get hurt again by others regardless of what I do. So the issue is, "What is the best response?" to these upcoming hurts so that I am not living in fear and being controlled by others.*

5. If I ignore it, the problem will go away. *The problem just gets buried and resurfaces later. Unresolved baggage from the past is brought into the present.*

6. Revenge: the person has to pay for it. He needs to be punished and learn a lesson. I want to hang on to the right to be a judge. *I'm not God, and trying to play God will get me in trouble. Vengeance belongs to the Lord.*

7. Failure to understand God's love and forgiveness for me. *I cannot give a gift to someone unless I first have something to give.*

8. Seems too easy and unfair. It seems I'm overlooking or condoning his sin. *No, in fact I am charging and documenting the debt and recognizing that Jesus died on the cross for that sin.*

9. Waiting for the person to come to me first. *It rarely happens.*

10. The person isn't sorry for what he's done. *Chances are he'll never be sorry. Forgiveness is primarily for my benefit. I don't need to wait.*

11. If I choose to forgive, I'm acting like a hypocrite because I don't "feel" loving and forgiving. *The truth is I'm a hypocrite if I don't forgive because my real nature in Christ is now a forgiving nature.*

12. Waiting for a "convenient" time and a "feeling." *It will never be convenient. I will never "feel" like forgiving.*

13. Thinking it takes too much time. I don't have time to forgive. *I can't afford **not** to forgive. I am the one in torment and in suffering.*

14. Fear of feelings that might be stirred up. *God knows how to gently get out the feelings that need to be healed. I won't die or go crazy.*

Freedom From Performance - Based Acceptance

But the Law does not rest on faith [does not require faith, has nothing to do with faith], for it itself says, He who does them [the things prescribed by the Law] shall live by them [not by faith].
Galatians 3:12 AMP

Lesson 8

A Life Transformed

During the summer after my third year of university studies, I was sitting in a Bible study when the leader showed a cartoon of a woman being taken to the insane asylum. Her pastor said to another member of the church, "We're really going to miss that woman. She did everything in this church."

Although I laughed with everyone else in the group, on the inside I felt like that woman. I was physically ill, emotionally drained, and spiritually dry because my life was so overloaded. I knew I couldn't continue to live the way I had been living ever since I was in high school. That's when I began to get the idea that I was loved and accepted only if I was successful. Although I didn't recognize this belief then, it began to affect my outlook on life.

I felt like I never measured up. I worked and worked, but I always felt that I needed to do one more thing to be really good. I wanted people to accept and approve of me, and I really wanted God's acceptance and approval, but I wasn't sure how to get it. I thought that God was disappointed in me and that He never totally approved of me. I carried a load of guilt and anxiety.

My belief that both people and God loved and accepted me because of my actions became even more dominant during my college years. I was very involved in the leadership of a Christian student organization, plus I was attending the university on an academic scholarship, and I was determined to graduate with a 4.0 GPA and honors.

I felt I would go crazy any minute.

to be continued...

Freedom From Performance-Based Acceptance — Lesson Eight

Performance-Based Acceptance

What is it, and where did it start?

Performance-Based Acceptance is common to mankind. It is behavior-driven and the environment in which we live and function. Whether it is in school, jobs or relationships it is how we try to gain love, acceptance and significance. We carry this into our relationship with God.

Performance-Based Acceptance started in the Garden of Eden with two trees.

> *And out of the ground the LORD God made every tree grow that is pleasant to the sight and good for food. The tree of life was also in the midst of the garden, and the tree of the knowledge of good and evil.* Genesis 2:9 NKJV

The command.

> *And the LORD God took the man and put him in the garden of Eden to tend and keep it. And the LORD God commanded the man, saying, "Of every tree of the garden you may freely eat; but of the tree of the knowledge of good and evil you shall not eat, for in the day that you eat of it you shall surely die."* Genesis 2:17-18 NKJV

The choice.

> *So when the woman saw that the tree was good for food, that it was pleasant to the eyes and a tree desirable to make one wise, she took of its fruit and ate. She also gave to her husband with her, and he ate.* Genesis 3:6 NKJV

Instead of living in a loving and dependent relationship with God, they chose to live independent of God living by their own self-effort and ability to judge good and evil. Another way to define this way of living is called "living from the flesh." From Adam and Eve, every human has been afflicted with this corrupted way of thinking. The tree of knowledge of good and evil could also be called the "tree of religion." Religion comes from the Latin word *religare* and means "to bind" as in the sense of placing an obligation on somebody (World Book Dictionary). Whether "flesh" or "religion," both refuse to acknowledge dependence on God and rely on self to determine good and evil for ourselves. If you do enough good, you will be loved, accepted and approved. If you do too much evil, you will disappoint God, others and

yourself. In the midst of failure we find ourselves filled with shame and can begin to believe God is ashamed of us. Fear enters in and we believe God is punishing or will punish us. In truth, the tree of knowledge of good and evil is simply the "tree of death." The enemy uses it to "steal, kill and destroy" John 10:10a. When we continue to live from this faulty thinking and partake of the tree of knowledge of good and evil, we will find ourselves in bondage to Performance-Based Acceptance to whomever or whatever we have given authority.

Attempting to live the Christian life based on Performance-Based Acceptance can cause many devastating problems:

- Physically – headaches, high blood pressure, fatigue, stomach disorders, digestive problems, sleep disorders.

- Behaviorally – critical spirit, workaholism, compulsive religious activity, chemical dependence, compulsive behaviors, perfectionism, high control, deeds of the flesh, suicide.

- Emotionally – stress, anger, fear of failure and punishment, guilt, anxiety, depression, hopelessness, despair, nervous breakdown.

- Mentally – poor concentration, chronic worrying, negativism, low self-esteem, self-condemnation, self-pity, lack of assurance of salvation, pride, judging, self-righteousness, wrong thinking about God, comparing self to others.

- Relationally – dependence on the approval of others, rejection of others who do not measure up, unresolved conflict, critical, angry.

The Guilt Trip

Another devastating problem caused by Performance-Based Acceptance is guilt. Guilt is recognized as one of the most painful and destructive emotions. Guilt is so universal and so deeply ingrained in human behavior that most of us accept it as a basic and normal emotion in our everyday experience. God desires to free His children from the bondage of guilt.

Guilt is recognized by the symptoms it produces.

- Self-condemnation: the constant blaming of oneself which can lead to depression.

- Self-punishment: a form of punishment inflicted upon oneself, usually to pay for some wrongdoing.

- Depression: the end result of guilt that hasn't been resolved

- Sense of Disapproval: the result of expectations of self or others that have not been met.

- Physical Symptoms: can include headaches, fatigue, and insomnia.

- Rationalization: an attempt to counteract guilt feelings by justifying one's actions.

- Compensation: another attempt to counteract guilt feelings by doing things considered to be good in an attempt to soothe the conscience.

- Anger: A feeling of hostility toward those who seem to stir up guilt feelings.

- Trying to Do Good: exemplary behavior which is often an attempt to conceal or deal with internal feelings of guilt.

- Fear and Dread: two closely related emotions, often associated with unresolved guilt feelings.

Christ As Life - Freedom

There was another tree in the midst of the garden, the tree of life. The first couple were never told they could not eat from that tree. The tree of life represents Christ and His life. Freedom from Performance-Based Acceptance and all its effects starts with awakening to the life of Christ and His righteousness within each believer.

> *Awake to righteousness, and do not sin* . . 1 Corinthians 15:34 NKJV

In Scripture, Jesus is called, "the second Adam" or the "second Man."

> *And so it is written, "The first man Adam became a living being." The last Adam became a life-giving spirit. . . . The first man was of the earth, made of dust; the second Man is the Lord from heaven.* 1 Corinthians 15:45, 47 NKJV

While the first Adam failed, the Second Adam succeeded. Christ came as a man and set right what had gone so wrong in the Garden of Eden. He came to set us free and to give us His life. We now have what Adam and Eve did not, the indwelling life of Christ, the fruit from the Tree of Life.

> *The Spirit of the LORD is upon Me, because He has anointed Me to preach the gospel to the poor; He has sent Me to heal the brokenhearted, to proclaim liberty to the captives and recovery of sight to the blind, to set at liberty those who are oppressed; to proclaim the acceptable year of the LORD.* Luke 4:18-19 NKJV

> *I am crucified with Christ: nevertheless I live; yet not I, but Christ liveth in me: and the life which I now live in the flesh I live by the faith of the Son of God, who loved me, and gave himself for me.* Galatians 2:20 KJV

Even though Christ came to set us free from Performance-Based Acceptance, we can still get caught up in the faulty thinking we must "do" to "become." This often happens because we hear a mixed message of Old and New Covenant. A message combining law and grace. At this point, it will be beneficial to look at the Old and New Covenants and see the difference between them.

Two Covenants

The English word *covenant* comes from the Latin *convenire*, and means "to come together or agree." The Hebrew word is *berith*, which means to "bind or to fetter; a binding obligation." In Scripture, it is the ultimate expression of committed love and trust and was usually made to define, confirm, establish, or make binding a relationship that had been in the making for some time.

There are two kinds of biblical covenants, conditional and unconditional. A conditional covenant is bilateral. It is a proposal of God to man and is characterized by, "if you will," then "I will." God promises to grant special blessings to man providing man fulfills certain conditions contained in the covenant and curses if he does not. Therefore, one's response to the covenant agreement brings either blessings or cursings.

An unconditional covenant is unilateral and is a sovereign act of God whereby He unconditionally obligates Himself to bring to pass definite blessings and conditions for the people in this covenant. This type is characterized by the "I wills" of God which declare His determination to do as He promises. Blessings are secured by the grace of God.

We will begin with a conditional, bilateral covenant.

The Old Covenant

The Old Covenant is also frequently referred to as "the Mosaic Covenant." It is also known as "the Law." It was conditional and based on "if you will, then I will." It focused on external behavior - performance. It was given **only** to the nation of Israel and makes up most of the first five books of the Bible. There were 613 laws, not just the Ten Commandments, contained in the Mosaic covenant. Also, contained in the covenant were blessings and promises. Failure to keep the covenant came with consequences. The purpose of the Law:

Copyright 1998, 2001, 2005, 2007, 2019, 2020 Scope Ministries International, INC.

1. Reveal the holy character of God;
2. Set apart Israel as distinct from other nations;
3. Reveal man's sinfulness;
4. Provide forgiveness through sacrifices;
5. Provide a way of worship;
6. Provide God's direction for their physical and spiritual health;
7. Cause people to see their failure and need for Christ, the Messiah; and
8. Prepare them for occupying the Promised Land.

Moses had led the children of Israel out of slavery in Egypt. They had seen God part the waters of the Red Sea and watched as the Egyptian army was drowned as the waters came back together. They traveled for three months and came to camp in the wilderness of Mt. Sinai. It was there Moses went up to God for He had chosen Moses to be His representative and the representative for the people. God spoke these words to Moses:

> *You have seen what I did to the Egyptians, and how I bore you on eagles' wings and brought you to Myself. Now therefore, if you will indeed obey My voice and keep My covenant, then you shall be a special treasure to Me above all people; for all the earth is Mine.* Exodus 19:4-5 NKJV

Moses told the people all the words of the LORD and all the judgments. The people responded with one voice.

> *All the words which the LORD has said we will do.* Exodus 24:3 NKJV.

Moses read them the covenant.

> *Then he took the Book of the Covenant and read in the hearing of the people. And they said, 'All that the LORD has said we will do and be obedient.' And Moses took the blood, sprinkled it on the people, and said, This is the blood of the covenant which the LORD has made with you according to all these words.* Exodus 24:7-8 NKJV

Israel's inability to keep the covenant shows up only a few chapters later. In Exodus 32, we read the story of the golden calf. Moses, acting as the representative, pleads with God on behalf of the people.

> *Then Moses pleaded with the LORD his God and said: 'LORD, why does Your wrath burn hot against Your people whom You have brought out of the land of Egypt with great power and with a mighty hand? Why should the Egyptians speak, and say 'He brought them out to harm them, to kill them in the mountains, and to consume them from the face of the earth?' Turn*

> *from Your fierce wrath and relent from this harm to Your people. Remember Abraham, Isaac, and Israel Your servants, to whom You swore by Your own self, and said to them, 'I will multiply your descendants as the stars of heaven; and all this land that I have spoken of I give to your descendants, and they inherit it forever.' So, the LORD relented from the harm which He said He would do to His people.* Exodus 32:11-14 NKJV

Throughout the story of the Israelites, we see a people unable to remain faithful, incapable of keeping their part of the covenant.

Their disobedience ultimately led the people into captivity. But even in their captivity, God remained faithful to them. He promised to bring them back to their own land.

> *Then you shall know that I am the LORD, when I have opened your graves, O My people, and brought you up from your graves. I will put My Spirit in you, and you shall live, and I will place you in your own land. Then you shall know that I, the LORD, have spoken it and performed it, says the LORD.* Ezekiel 37:13-14 NKJV

God brings them back to their own land and at the time of the writing of Malachi, Israel is one nation living under the domination of Persia. There are 400 years between Malachi and Matthew.

The New Covenant

The Greek word *diatheke* is often translated either "covenant" or "testament." When did the Mosaic Covenant (the Old Covenant) end? When did the New Covenant start? It would be common to think the Old Covenant (Testament) ends with the beginning of Matthew. However, when you consider the word "testament" what do you think of? You may think of a last will and testament. Which is exactly right. When does a will and testament go into effect? Only at the death of the testator! The New Testament or New Covenant begins at the death of Christ not at His birth.

Christ was born under the Law.

> *But when the fullness of time had come, God sent forth His Son, born of a woman, born under the law, to redeem those who were under the law, that we might receive the adoption as sons.* Galatians 4:4 NKJV

Jesus made it clear He came for the Jews. They were the ones under the Mosaic Covenant, the Law. Gentiles were not included in the Mosaic Covenant. The Law did not apply to them and it does not apply to us today. See, Matthew 15:24.

When Jesus taught the Jewish people, He interpreted and taught the Law perfectly, thereby fulfilling the Law. Consider Jesus' words in Matthew 5:27-28 NKJV.

> *You have heard that it was said to those of old, 'You shall not commit adultery.' But I say to you that whoever looks at a woman to lust for her has already committed adultery with her in his heart.*

To the scribes and Pharisees, the ones who thought they were keeping the Law perfectly He had these words:

> *Woe to you, scribes and Pharisees, hypocrites! For you cleanse the outside of the cup and dish, but inside they are full of extortion and self-indulgence. Blind Pharisee, first cleanse the inside of the cup and dish, that the outside of them may be clean also. Woe to you scribes and Pharisees, hypocrites! For you are like whitewashed tombs which indeed appear beautiful outwardly, but inside are full of dead men's bones and all uncleanness. Even so you also outwardly appear righteous to men, but inside you are full of hypocrisy and lawlessness.* Matthew 23:25-28 NKJV

Jesus was not giving them a new standard to live up to, He was giving them an impossible standard to keep. By interpreting and teaching the Law correctly, He increased their burden. Christ came to the Jews to show them they needed something only He could provide – life! They were dead in their trespasses and sin and no matter how good they looked on the outside, they were dead on the inside. The Law could not give life or make them righteous. If it could have, Jesus would have died in vain. Jesus said,

> *I am the way, the truth and the life. No one comes to the Father except through Me.* John 14:6 NKJV

Christ took away the old and established the new

Before the New Covenant was established, the first had to be taken away.

> *then He said, "Behold, I have to do Your will, O God." He takes away the first that He may establish the second.* Hebrews 10:9 NKJV

At the Last Supper and before His death, Jesus spoke these words:

> *For this is My blood of the new covenant, which is shed for many for the remission of sins.* Matthew 26:28 NKJV

The phrase "takes away" means to take away violently, as in death or murder. So, how did Christ take away the first? With His death! Jesus said, "It is finished." The work of redemption was finished and so was the Law. The "second" was established by His resurrection and sending of

Holy Spirit to live in us. This fulfilled the prophecy found in Ezekiel 36:26 NKJV.

> *I will give you a new heart and put a new spirit within you. I will take the heart of stone out of your flesh and give you a heart of flesh. I will put My Spirit within you and cause you to walk in My statutes, and you will keep My judgments and do them.*

The New Covenant is not a system of performance and self-effort, but one of reliance and rest based on Christ and His finished work. Believers now have the indwelling life of Christ by Holy Spirit. This new way to live is called, "living by grace." The fruit of the Spirit is not a work we do, but a natural occurrence as we live in, rest and rely on Holy Spirit. His fruit is the life of Christ seen in us.

> *But the fruit of the Spirit is love, joy, peace, longsuffering, kindness, goodness, faithfulness, gentleness, self-control. Against such there is no law.* Galatians 5:22-23 NKJV.

We encourage you when reading the Old Testament and the gospels, you read it through the lens of the finished work of Jesus Christ and the New Covenant. When we mix the Old Covenant with the New we put ourselves in bondage and are unable to benefit from the freedom Christ has given us.

> *So Christ has truly set us free. Now make sure that you stay free, and don't get tied up again in slavery to the law.* Galatians 5:1 NLT.

To summarize: The New Covenant and Grace are a Person – Jesus Christ!

Benefits of living out of the New Covenant

You read the effects of living under The Old Covenant of the Law and the bondage of performance and the resulting guilt it produces. What is the difference in living out of the New Covenant and Grace? The following chart sets out the differences and will help us to see the benefits of living in Grace.

Old Covenant of the Law	New Covenant of Grace
Given by God to Moses. John 1:17	Accomplished and realized through Christ. John 1:17
Written on stone. Deuteronomy 4:13	Written on our hearts. 2 Corinthians 3:2-3
Sheep died for sin. Exodus 12:21	The Shepherd (the Lamb) died. John 10:11, John 1:29
Had an end. Romans 10:4; Hebrews 10:9	Has no end. Ephesians 2:6-7
Obedience to become. Luke 18:18	Christ is our obedience. Philippians 2:8
Produces self-righteousness and pride. Luke 18:9-14	We have Christ's righteousness Philippians 3:8-9; 2 Corinthians 5:21
Ministry of condemnation and guilt. 2 Corinthians 3:9	Ministry of forgiveness and reconciliation. 2 Corinthians 5:17-19; Ephesians 1:7, 4:32
Promotes separation.	Gives oneness, glory, love and intimacy with God. John 17:20-23
Requires perfect performance. James 2:10	Christ fulfilled the Law for us and as us. Romans 5:15-17
Powerless over sin. Colossians 2:20-23	Takes away sin. Psalm 103:12. Forgiven once for all; past, present and future. Hebrews 10:1-18
Bondage. Galatians 3:22	Freedom. Galatians 5:1
Punishment. 1 John 4:18	Peace. 1 John 4:18
Shame and guilt.	Confidence. Philippians 1:6
Identified as a "sinner."	New identity, partaker of the divine nature. A saint. 2 Peter 1:4; Ephesians 1:1
Living by the Law creates a performance consciousness, focusing on self. This drains us of spiritual life and robs us of joy and peace.	Living under the New Covenant and dependence on Holy Spirit creates a God consciousness, focusing on who He is and what He has done for us. This causes us to respond to His love and to worship Him, resulting in joy and peace in our life.
Working to be accepted by God. Because our performance is always imperfect, we never feel completely accepted by God. We live from a position of weakness, because we work to be accepted, but never achieve it.	Relying on Christ as our Source. The Spirit bears witness with our spirit that we are accepted by God through the merit of Christ. By relying solely on His righteousness, we know we are accepted by Him. We live from a position of strength, because we have been made acceptable.
Living by the Law leads to further sin and failure because we are walking according to the flesh (self-effort). Galatians 5:6-21	Walking by the Spirit produces freedom and victory over sin and the life of Christ (fruit of the Spirit) is produced in our life. Galatians 5:22-25
A day of Sabbath rest. Exodus 20:8-11	A life of Sabbath Rest. Hebrews 4:9

Summary:

Living free of Performance-Based Acceptance, we are now enabled by Holy Spirit to live:

- Forgiven - No more keeping track of sin. ALL sin has been removed from us as far as the east is from the west. When we allow ourselves to live forgiven, knowing God is not keeping track of our sin, we then experience the ability to forgive others.

- Free – No longer a victim of shame and guilt. Jesus took our shame and guilt and gave us His glory. John 17:22

- In rest – Living from Christ as our Life and Source. Hebrews 4:9

- In His Supply – We are no longer our own Source, but from Christ who is everything we need for life and godliness. 2 Peter 1:3

- In Peace – To know Jesus as Peace and He will never leave or forsake us. Hebrews 13:5 AMP

- In Oneness – Experiencing the oneness Christ promised. John 17:21

- Confident – Being confident the good Christ has started in us will be completed. Philippians 1:6

- With no fear – Jesus, who is Perfect love, casts out fear. 1 John 4:18

- Assured – Holy Spirit testifies to our spirits we are God's children. Romans 8:16

- As a conqueror – In all things we are more than conquerors. Romans 8:37

- Loved – We are loved by the Father as He loved Jesus. John 17:23

- As a joint-heir with Christ – Romans 8:17

- As a partaker of the divine nature – We now have a new identity. 2 Peter 1:4

> A Life Transformed, cont.
>
> My last year at the university, I began to learn about my identity in Christ. I realized that God doesn't look at what I do, but cares about who I am. I discovered that I didn't understand God's character. In a Bible study we talked about legalism and standards. Things began to change in my life.
>
> God showed me that Christian activities are never a replacement for having faith in Him to lead me and complete me.
>
> I saw that I needed to believe that God loves and accepts me just the way I am and He will lead me to mature in Christ. One thing I did was to ask Him what committments He wanted me to commit to. To my surprize He showed me things to drop and things to add.
>
> I realized that I had done some activities to please God, but now I "wanted to" instead of "having to."
>
> My life did not change instantly. Even now, I sometimes hear a voice in the back of my mind telling me that I am guilty and that I still don't measure up, but now I know the truth. I can answer the voice with the certainty that God is working in me. As I listen to His Holy Spirit, He guides me into the places and situations He has planned for me. I don't need to constantly seek ways to measure my worth. God has relieved me of a huge burden and replaced it with great love and His joy.
>
> Julianna - Teacher

Freedom From Performance-Based Acceptance
Day One

Goal: To understand the purpose of God's Law and to recognize how I might be misusing it in my life.

1. Complete the following statements:

    God would be more pleased with me if . . .

    I would be a good/better Christian if I could . . .

    I feel God expects me to . . .

    God is disappointed with me when I . . .

    Your answers to these questions may reveal that you are still trying to be "good enough" to go to Heaven or to be loved and accepted by God.

    The Law (of the Old Testament) is an objective external standard that expresses the expectations of a righteous and holy God. Jesus summarized the Law with two commands: "Love the Lord your God" and "Love your neighbor as yourself." The Law reveals what this should look like in human behavior.

2. What do each of the following verses reveal concerning the purpose of God's Law?

    Now we recognize and know that the Law is good if any one uses it lawfully [for the purpose for which it was designed], Knowing and understanding this: that the Law is not enacted for the righteous (the upright and just, who are in right standing with God), but for the lawless and unruly, for the ungodly and sinful . . .
    1 Timothy 1:8-9a Amplified

    What then was the purpose of the Law? It was added [later on, after the promise, to disclose and expose to men their guilt] because of transgressions and [to make men more conscious of the sinfulness] of sin.. . . .
    Galatians 3:19 Amplified

    So that the Law served [to us Jews] as our trainer [our guardian, our guide to Christ, to lead us] until Christ [came], that we might be justified (declared righteous, put in right standing with God) by and through faith.   Galatians 3:24 Amplified

> *If you seek to be justified and declared righteous and to be given a right standing with God through the Law, you are brought to nothing and so separated (severed) from Christ. You have fallen away from grace (from God's gracious favor and unmerited blessing).   Galatians 5:4 AMP*

The Law is not the Gospel. The Law was intended to be a "thermometer, not a thermostat." It reveals our standing in relationship to God's standards, but it does not make us capable of gaining or achieving those standards. The main purpose of the Law is to reveal to us God's holiness and our need of Him.

3. Read Romans 7:5-8.

What is aroused by the Law?

How are we released from the Law? What does the Law show you?

The Gospel is the good news about God's grace in response to man's sin (failure to love God and others). The word "grace" means, "that which causes joy, pleasure, gratification, favor, acceptance. A favor done without expectation of return; the absolute freeness of the loving kindness of God to men finding its only motive in the bounty and benevolence of the Giver; unearned and unmerited favor." (Spiros Zodhiates, The Complete Word Study Dictionary)

> *For it is by free grace (God's unmerited favor) that you are saved (delivered from judgment and made partakers of Christ's salvation) through [your] faith. And this [salvation] is not of yourselves [of your own doing, it came not through your own striving], but it is the gift of God; not because of works [not the fulfillment of the Law's demands], lest any man should boast. [It is not the result of what anyone can possibly do, so no one can pride himself in it or take glory to himself].   Ephesians 2:8-9 Amplified*

4. Spend a few minutes expressing gratitude to God for the free gift of salvation by personalizing and praying the verse above.

Freedom From Performance-Based Acceptance
Day Two

Goal: To evaluate how I'm trying to meet my needs for acceptance and approval and to receive God's acceptance and approval of me.

If you are already convinced that you are saved by grace and not through keeping the Law, can you still be living on the "performance treadmill?" You are if you are trying to gain approval and acceptance from God, others, or self through keeping the Law or standards.

1. To discover if this is true, look at question 1 of Day One. What do your answers reveal?

2. How are you trying or what are you trying to do to gain God's acceptance and approval?

3. In what areas do you feel unaccepted by God? Do you feel unaccepted because you have failed to keep God's commands or because you have believed a lie about yourself or God?

4. What do the following verses tell you about your acceptance and approval by God?

> *Yet now has [Christ, the Messiah,] reconciled [you to God] in the body of His flesh through death, in order to present you holy and faultless and irreproachable in His [the Father's] presence.*
> Colossians 1:22 Amplified

Therefore, [there is] now no condemnation (no judging guilty of wrong) for those who are in Christ Jesus.
Romans 8:1 *Amplified*

Even as [in His love] He chose us - [actually picked us out for Himself as His own], in Christ before the foundation of the world; that we should be holy (consecrated and set apart for Him) and blameless in His sight, even above reproach, before Him in love.
Ephesians 1:4 AMP

Wherefore, accept one another, just as Christ also accepted us to the glory of God.
Romans 15:7 NASB

5. God's approval and acceptance of us is not based on our performance but on who we are: His Spirit-born children. Choose to accept by faith what God says in His Word and to receive God's approval and acceptance of you. Write Him a thank-you note.

Freedom From Performance-Based Acceptance
Day Three

Goal: To recognize any standards I am living by and learn what it means to walk by the Spirit.

Many times, we feel that we have to "stick to the rules" or "maintain certain standards" in order to make sure we live a Godly life and are accepted by others. We may fear that we will lose control of our life if we cease trying to achieve our standards. However, the truth is that living by self-imposed rules has absolutely no value in "restraining sensual indulgences" (the flesh). In fact, according to Romans 7, rules actually arouse sin!

> *But sin, finding opportunity in the commandment [to express itself], got a hold on me and aroused and stimulated all kinds of forbidden desires (lust, covetousness). For without the Law sin is dead [the sense of it is inactive and a lifeless thing]. Romans 7:8 AMP*

> *For sin, seizing the opportunity and getting a hold on me [by taking its incentive] from the commandment, beguiled and entrapped and cheated me, and using it [as a weapon], killed me. Romans 7:11 AMP*

1. As you grew up, what were some of the family rules or standards (spoken or unspoken) that you were expected to live up to?

2. What are some of your church's standards that you feel you need to meet in order to be considered a "good Christian?"

3. List a standard you use to judge whether others are acceptable or worthy. (Hint: What are your pet peeves? When others don't conform, do you become angry?)

4. According to Colossians 2:20-23, living by standards and Laws appears to be beneficial, but actually has no profit (does not make us loving in our actions or attitudes). In your relationships, what are some of the negative consequences of living by the Law or standards?

5. Make a list of your standards that you have used to measure your worth or to gain acceptance. One by one, give your standards to God, acknowledging that living by your standards will never empower you to love God or others. Thank God that they are not His demands on you.

6. Ask God to teach you how to "walk by the Spirit" rather than walking in the "flesh" (living by Laws and standards). Meditate on the following verse and on what it means in your daily life. Write on a 3 x 5 card or sticky note, and put it where you will see it often.

> *I have been crucified with Christ; and it is no longer I who live, but Christ lives in me; and the life which I now live in the flesh I live by faith in the Son of God, who loved me, and delivered Himself up for me. I do not nullify the grace of God; for if righteousness comes through the Law, then Christ died needlessly.*
> Galatians 2:20-21 NAS

Freedom From Performance-Based Acceptance
Day Four

Goal: To discover the difference between living on the performance treadmill and living and walking in the freedom of the Spirit.

1. Read Galatians 3:2-3. What is your part in living by the Spirit?

Rather than living by external rules, we are to live and walk by the Spirit, responding in faith to His inner prompting. "Walk" speaks of a continuous process, a moment-by-moment dependence on the Holy Spirit. Our part is to respond to His leading, and God's part is to empower us with His supernatural life.

Jesus invites all who are tired, exhausted, and frustrated from trying to live the "Christian" life by their own efforts to come to Him and rest. The word "rest" means to cease from living the Christian life by self-effort. It is putting our faith in Jesus and allowing Him to live His life through us.

> *Come to Me, all you who labor and are heavy-laden and overburdened, and I will cause you to rest. [I will ease and relieve and refresh your souls.] Take My yoke upon you and learn of Me, for I am gentle (meek) and humble (lowly) in heart, and you will find rest (relief and ease and refreshment and recreation and blessed quiet) for your souls. For My yoke is wholesome (useful, good—not harsh, hard, sharp, or pressing, but comfortable, gracious, and pleasant), and My burden is light and easy to be borne.*
> Matthew 11:28-30 Amplified

2. List some of your "red flags" (indicators) that tell you that you are not "resting" in Jesus (trusting Him to live through you).

Examples:
• I become anxious and stressed about all I have to do.
• I think that God is disgusted or disappointed with me for some failure in my life (and I feel shame and condemnation).

3. For each of the examples you listed above, describe how you could "rest" in Jesus?

Examples:
• When I am stressed, cast all my worries on Him. Give Him my list of things to do, as well as my expectations, and trust Him to empower me and direct my day.
• When I fail, agree with God concerning my sin and thank Him that He has not only forgiven me, but made me acceptable. Choose to renew my mind with the truth about my new identity and trust the Holy Spirit to empower me to do what is right.

4. Look back at your answers on Day One Lesson 1 "The Truth About Lies." In what ways are the problem(s) you described a result of living by your own standards or self-effort instead of relying on the Holy Spirit?

5. Personalize Matthew 11:28-30 as your pray, trusting in Jesus to give you rest from your self-effort and to empower you through His Spirit.

Example:
"Jesus, I am tired and weary of trying to do things for You and trying to please others. Thank You Jesus for inviting me to come to You to find rest. I am exhausted from trying to live the Christian life through self-effort. Teach me what it means to rest in You and depend on Your Spirit in my daily life."

Freedom From Performance-Based Acceptance
Day Five

Goal: To recognize and heal emotional guilt.

1. Check below the symptoms of emotional guilt which you recognize in your life. Write one reason why you feel guilty and how you experience this guilt.

- Self-condemnation: the constant blaming of oneself. This can lead to depression.

- Self-punishment: any form of punishment which is inflicted upon oneself, usually to pay for some wrongdoing.

- Depression: The end result of guilt that hasn't been addressed.

- Sense of Disapproval: The result of expectations of yourself or others that have not been met.

- Physical Symptoms: can include headaches, fatigue, and insomnia.

- Rationalization: an attempt to justify one's actions to counter guilt feelings.

- Compensation: An attempt to soothe the conscience by doing things considered to be good. Another attempt to counter guilt feelings.

- Anger: A feeling of hostility toward those who seem to prompt guilt feelings.

- "Goody Two-Shoes:" Exemplary behavior which is often another attempt to mask internal guilt feelings.

- Fear and Dread: Two closely related emotions which are often associated with unresolved guilt feelings.

2. For each example you wrote above, confess (agree with God; give thanks) concerning His complete forgiveness of you and for giving you the righteousness of Christ.

Freedom From Performance-Based Acceptance
Summary

Name

Date

Answer the following questions. To turn in page to small group leader.

1. How is living on the "Performance-Based Acceptance" evident in your life?

2. What laws or standards have you tried to live up to in order to earn God's approval and acceptance? What has been the result of living by these laws or standards?

3. What standards have you tried to live up to in order to gain a sense of self-worth or to get approval and acceptance from others?

4. How has living on the "Performance-Based Acceptance" affected the quality of your life? Your relationship with God? With others?

5. What is your understanding of how you are to live the Christian life?

6. Mark the graph to indicate how much of this week's assignment you completed.

0 ———————————————— 50% ———————————————— 100%

A Life Transformed

But we all, with unveiled face beholding as in a mirror the glory of the Lord, are being transformed into the same image from glory to glory, just as from the Lord, the Spirit.
2 Corinthians 3:18 NASB

Lesson 9

A Life Transformed

I was one of those people who always did my best. I always gave 110% because I wanted everything in my life and everyone else's life to run smoothly. I knew that I could run the world if everyone would do just what I told them.

Despite all my efforts to keep my marriage together, it was falling apart. I was miserable. I had reached the end of my rope and knew that I could not continue the way I was and still survive. Of course, I thought that things would be fine again if my husband Jeff would change.

I turned to God looking for ways to fix Jeff and my marriage but instead, I found the way to allow God to change me and to mend my relationship with Him. He taught me that my ability to handle the challenges in my life depends upon my relationship with Him and how I view Him.

I had always related to people in my life by performing, and I thought that I had to relate to God as a performer too. I had many fears of being close to God because that meant more things to do and more tasks to complete. When I didn't meet what I imagined were God's expectations, I thought that He was punishing me by allowing my marriage to fail.

I discovered that my identity is based on what God has done for me, not what I have done for Him. I was so relieved to know that God cares for me the same no matter what I was doing or experiencing in my life. He wants to care for me and assume control of my life, but giving up that control to God was very difficult for me because I thought that I knew what was best. I learned that my greatest weakness was my independence from God. God's goals for my life are that I am closer to Him, That I am more like Him, that I depend upon Him, and that I find my worth, value, and identity throught Him.

I thought I had mastered these concepts and I was feeling pleased with myself. I was doing the right things, so I expected God to fix my marriage, but Jeff and I reached another crisis point, and my world began to fall apart again. I realized that even as I had applied these principles to my life. I was still trying to stay in control. I had given God all my options, and I expected Him to pick one. I finally let go.

to be continued . . .

A Life Transformed - Lesson Nine

Through the past eight lessons we have laid a foundation for experiencing a transformed life. We have discovered some of our faulty beliefs about the Gospel, who we are, Who God is, and the Spirit-filled life. We have also identified some of the obstacles to experiencing the truth of what God has done in our lives. We have recognized that the presenting problem is merely the symptom of a deeper problem: our faulty beliefs which keep us from relating to God as He really is. This final lesson will help us understand how all of life is connected to our relationship with God.

Life's Problems are often our Motivation to Seek God

Without life's problems, we wouldn't recognize our need to know and relate to God personally. Our problems and our failures become the environment in which we can experience and appreciate Who God really is. If we do not recognize and acknowledge failure, we wouldn't understand God's unconditional love and acceptance. Also we couldn't experience God's character. His grace would have little meaning. Those who have come to know God are often motivated to seek God by His indwelling Holy Spirit. Remember, a believer's focus is on the source of all of life - Jesus Who provides all that we need including victory over problems.

The following chart is a summary of each of the root problems we have identified in the previous lessons and the solution to each of them.

A Life Transformed

The Problem	The Solution
1. Our belief system is faulty. Proverbs 14:12; 23:7a	Renewing our minds allows the Spirit to transform our lives. John 8:31-32; Romans 12:2
2. Being born without knowledge of God causes us to be dysfunctional as human beings. Not understanding the implications of the Gospel makes us dysfunctional as God's children. Ephesians 2:1-3	Through faith in Jesus Christ we are reconciled to God and receive His Eternal Life. We can experience God's quality of life now. John 5:24; Colossians 1:19-20
3. The memory of our old identity causes us to live in defeat and in bondage to the flesh. Romans 7:17-18	Believing the truth of our new identity and depending on the Holy Spirit gives us victory over the flesh. 2 Corinthians 5:16-17; Colossians 3:9-10
4. Our faulty view of God robs us of joy and intimacy in our relationship with Him and keeps us from growing in our spiritual lives. John 6:46	Seeing the Father through Jesus and seeing ourselves as His deeply loved children frees us to rest in God's unconditional love. John 1:18, 14:6-9; 1 John 3:1-2
5. Living independently of God leads to self-sufficiency and to trying to live the Christian life in our own strength. This does not produce real life. Philippians 3:3-4	Having been filled and led by His Spirit results in a productive life filled with joy and peace. John 7:38; Galatians 5:16; Ephesians 5:18-19
6. Our emotions become our final authority, controlling what we believe and the choices we make.	Expressing emotions to God (REED) and making the Living and Written Word the final authority for what we believe. This results in greater intimacy with God and viewing life from God's perspective. Psalm 34:4; 1 Peter 5:7
7. Unresolved anger produces unforgiveness and bitterness (which destroys relationships) and eventually depression. 2 Peter 1:9; Hebrews 12:15	Agreeing with God concerning forgiveness, applying forgiveness by releasing others and extending God's forgiveness toward them leads to freedom. Romans 12:1; Colossians 2:13-14, 3:13
8. Motivation by guilt results in a performance-based Christian life. We work hard to try to earn our salvation, spirituality, acceptance, and worth. Our efforts to improve the flesh produces only more failure. Galatians 3:2-3, 10	Receive God's unconditional love and grace while resting in Christ for our acceptance and worth, we depend on the Holy Spirit as He lives through us. Galatians 2:19-20; 3:2; Ephesians 2:8-9

Everything we've covered has led us to the core issue of life, which is:

The Problem	The Solution
9. Our faulty view of God leads us to worship people and things, resulting in bondage to fear and all sorts of evil. Romans 1:25-32	Worshipping God for Who He really is results in abundant and transformed life in the midst of life's problems. John 4:23-24; 2 Corinthians 3:18

Right worship leads to a transformed life

Ultimately all of life depends upon the answer to the question, "Who is my God?" As beings created to worship, we will worship something or someone. We become like the one we worship (Acts 4:13). Worship simply means "worth - ship." When we worship something or someone, we are believing in its superior value and worth. The dictionary defines "worship" as "giving reverence, honor and devotion; to be full of adoration."

We worship what we view as most important and vital to life. We depend upon what or who we worship. For example: If we believe money or possessions are the source of worth and value and are vital for life, then we are worshipping money. If we believe our family is what is most important and vital to life, then we are worshipping our family. To worship God rightly means that we view Him as the most vital, important, and worthy person in our lives. Only when we recognize God for Who He really is can we rightly worship Him. Only as we begin to worship God for Who He truly is can we see ourselves as we really are. Right worship of God allows us to experience our new identity in our daily lives and to be a blessing to others.

God reveals Himself in the midst of life's problems

We can know God only because He chooses to make Himself known. Our needs and problems become an opportunity for God to make Himself known to us experientially. God can be seen and experienced best in the midst of life's problems.

- Obstacles become opportunities to see God overcome;
- In pain and loss, we receive God's comfort;
- Our weakness gives way to His strength;
- Our lack brings God's supply;
- Through our trials we experience Him as our deliverer;
- In our failure we receive His grace;
- In our defeat He becomes our Victory;
- In times of stress and turmoil He gives us peace;
- During times of sorrow He gives us His joy; and
- When we are rejected, He fills our hearts with His unconditional love.

By letting God be Who He is in us, we become outwardly whom God has already made us inwardly in Christ. One of the most important things God wants to do in us is to

renew our minds with the TRUTH of Who He is and who He has made us to be.

Through right worship of God we can see ourselves as God sees us, created in His image. He is the Source of everything we need for life and Godliness. When we are rightly connected to God, we can then see life from His perspective.

We are living, thinking, believing, worshipping beings

Scripture addresses us on all four levels:

- as a **living** being (our behavior and emotions);
- as a **thinking** being (our thoughts and reasoning);
- as a **believing** being (our beliefs, values, and convictions);
- as a **worshipping** being (our spiritual nature and relationship with God).

To address our problems from God's perspective, we need to address all four of these areas. At times, we need to deal with our emotions and what they are telling us about what we are thinking and believing. But we also need to identify the root issue in order to expose our wrong perception of God (which can result in idolatry) and to see God as the loving, trustworthy Father that He is. By acknowledging our wrong beliefs at this level, we can begin to worship God in spirit and in truth. Through right worship of God, we are transformed into His likeness a little at a time.

The funnel chart below is a visual example of the relationship between the four levels of our experience and our view of God. Before we can permanently and effectively address our behavior, emotions, thoughts, and beliefs, we must deal with Who God is to us personally. Some change is possible without addressing this root issue; however, no permanent change is possible without growing in an intimate relationship with our Creator.

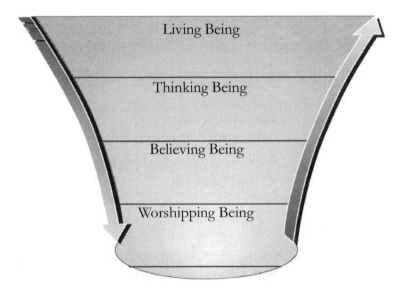

The living level

Working down the left side of the funnel chart, we first record what is happening on the "living" level. In other words, how are we responding in our behavior and emotions to the presenting problem?

The thinking level

Our behavior and emotions tell us something about what is happening in our thought processes, which is the rational level. Here we record what we are actually thinking about the problem or issue being addressed.

The believing level

Our thoughts then reveal what we are really believing in that particular situation. This level reveals our beliefs about ourselves, which control how we respond to life situations. It also reveals the standards by which we are living.

The worshipping level

Our beliefs define what we really believe about God, because generally, how we think God views us is what we also believe about ourselves. This reveals how we are really viewing God in this situation.

> *But we all, with unveiled face beholding as in a mirror the glory of the Lord, are being transformed into the same image from glory to glory, just as from the Lord, the Spirit.*
> 2 Corinthians 3:18 NASB

By working down the left side of the chart, we discover our wrong beliefs about God. Then we can begin putting off the old way of viewing God and putting on the new. To work back up the right side of the funnel, we start at the worshipping level and begin to look to the Living and Written Word to know what is really true about God. We compare the things we believe about God on the left side with the Word, writing the Scripture verses that address the wrong beliefs. First, we need to acknowledge to God the way we have viewed Him, and then choose to reject the lies we have believed about Him. Finally, we thank God for Who He really is and ask Him to make Himself known in this way.

On the believing level, we accept the truth about God and proclaim that what is true about us is based on Who God is and Who He has made us to be in our new identity. We reject and renounce the lies we have believed about ourselves and put on the truth of who we are in Christ. As a new creation, we choose to see ourselves as God sees us. Again we thank God for changing us and giving us His nature. Because God is love, we are loved and able to love others. We understand that we are able only because He is able. We give out of what we have received from Him.

On the thinking level, we write the thoughts that will result from our new beliefs about God and about who we are in Christ. As Philippians 4:8 tells us, we choose to think about those things that are true, honorable, right, pure, lovely, attractive, excellent, and worthy of praise. We choose to think about our problems and circumstances from God's perspective, rejoicing in the Lord and giving thanks in everything. We set our thoughts on the thoughts from the Spirit instead of on the memory of the old way of life.

Copyright 1998, 2001, 2005, 2007, 2019, 2020 Scope Ministries International, INC.

On the living level, we write the behaviors and emotions that will result from our renewed beliefs and thoughts about God and ourselves. Remember, our feelings are the last to change. We acknowledge any sinful patterns of behavior that have resulted from our false beliefs about God and ourselves. We then act on our new beliefs and thoughts. As we make right choices, our feelings will eventually change. We choose to live by faith rather than by what we perceive with our physical senses. As we talk to God about everything, He will continue to reveal Himself to us, giving us His perspective of life.

Our Purpose Is Not to Avoid Problems, But to Know God

Renewing our minds is a process which involves changing our purpose and goal in life. Because our purpose is to be the friend and companion of God and to reflect His character, our goal is to know God experientially as He really is. This involves our viewing God as our most vital necessity in life. Our need to know God is more important than our earthly relationships, worldly possessions, and temporal pleasures. Delighting in the Lord and relating to Him in the midst of our personal struggles will result in a transformed life.

The solution to any problem is found in knowing and relating to God

We can use the tools received from this study to address our problems from God's perspective, and not just our present problems, but also our future ones.

> And this is eternal life, that they may know Thee, the only true God, and Jesus Christ whom Thou has sent.   John 17:3 NAS

> *Seeing that His divine power has granted to us everything pertaining to life and Godliness, through the true knowledge of Him Who called us by His own glory and excellence. For by these He has granted to us His precious and magnificent promises, in order that by them you might become partakers of the divine nature, having escaped the corruption that is in the world by lust.* 2 Peter 1:3-4 NASB

Our part is to seek. to know. and relate to God in the midst of life's problems

Seeking to know God requires being open and honest with God concerning our beliefs and behaviors. This requires the personal involvement of our mind, will, and emotions. Without the involvement of all three, we will not experience a fully personal relationship. To get to know another person, we have to be in each other's company and be open and transparent with one another. God has taken the initiative to make Himself known to us through His Word and His Son. He loved us before the foundation of the world. What matters most is not that we know God, but that He knows us.

- We are tattooed on the palm of His hands. (Isaiah 49:16)
- We are never out of His mind. (Psalm 139:17-18; Psalm 40:5)
- He knows the very number of hairs on our head. (Matthew 10:30)
- He saves all our tears in His bottle. (Psalm 56:8)
- He knows us as a Father, and there is no moment when His eye is off us or His attention distracted from us. Therefore, there is no moment when His care falters. (Luke 12:6-7)

It is a tremendous relief to know that God's love for us is totally realistic and is based, at every point, on prior knowledge of the worst about us. There is no discovery that can disillusion Him about us or quench His determination to bless us. When we realize that He sees all the twisted things about us that even others do not see, He looks beyond the outer man and sees the new person He has created us to be, there is no room for pride. The knowledge of His unconditional love and acceptance of us creates in us the desire to worship, adore, and love God with all our heart, mind, soul, and strength.

Intimacy With God Results in an Abundant Life

We must address any obstacles to our experiencing intimacty with God.

These nine lessons were designed to help you recognize and address the obstacles that may be limiting your intimacy with God. To experience intimacy with any person, we need a correct view of ourselves and of the other person. This is the primary reason why lessons three, The Truth About Your New Identity, four, The Truth About the Heavenly Father, are so critical. Consider this question: Do you want a close relationship with someone who you think …

- Is untrustworthy?
- Does not care about you?
- Merely tolerates your presence?
- Gets mad at you when you fail?
- Loves you only when you perform well?

You can complete this list with any of the false beliefs the Holy Spirit revealed to you about God in lesson four. You must address these false beliefs if you are going to experience God as He truly is. If you have an accurate view of God, you will desire intimacy with Him. Any false belief about God will limit your intimacy with Him, because it will give you a concept of God less than He really is. It is impossible for you to believe He is more loving than He is. He is love personified! Likewise, it is impossible for you to believe He is more good, more holy, more forgiving, or more anything than He is.

Consider this question: Do you want a close relationship with someone if you think …

- You are unacceptable?
- You are going to be rejected if the other person really gets to know you?
- You will never meet the other person's standards?
- You will be condemned by the other person?

You can complete this list with any of the false beliefs you identified about yourself from lesson three - The Truth About Your New Identity on page 63. Any one of these beliefs will hinder you from developing an intimate relationship with God.

Why is an intimate relationship with God so important? It is only within this relationship that you will experience abundant life—God's quality of life which has been given to us through Christ.

The abundant life that Jesus promised you is not contingent on your circumstances. He did not say, "I came that you might have life and have it abundantly if your marriage is fulfilling,

It is impossible to believe that God is more loving that He really is.

your bills are paid, your past is not filled with pain, etc." No one is excluded from Jesus' promise of abundant life. You can experience it, regardless of your circumstances, because you experience it as you experience God in the midst of your circumstances.

Only God can meet all your needs

God revealed Himself to Moses as "I AM WHO I AM." Think of your current needs, and fill in God's revelation of Himself: "I AM" (whatever you need). Your Abba Father loves you deeply and longs to meet your needs.

Often we do not experience Him as "I AM," because we turn to other sources to meet our needs. God expressed this through Jeremiah when He said,

> For My people have committed two evils: They have forsaken Me, the fountain of living waters, to hew for themselves cisterns, broken cisterns, that can hold no water. Jeremiah 2:13 NASB

Like the people of Jeremiah's day, we are not turning to God, the only fountain of Living Water, to meet our needs. Rather, we have used our own means to meet our needs. But as Jeremiah wrote, our methods are "broken" and ineffective. Will you choose today to begin seeking your loving Abba Father to meet the needs of your life? He longs to do so, and He is the only one Who truly can.

We have only just begun

Seeking to know God is a lifelong process

God desires for us to continue the discovery process. Don't set this workbook aside, but use it as a reference tool when facing future problems. Review and re-ask the personal application questions when encountering a new problem. The list on page 85 in the lesson 3 The Truth about Your New Identity and the list of characteristics described in lesson 4 The Truth About the Heavenly Father can be wonderful Bible studies. Use the "REED" lesson (page 146 in the lesson Freedom with Emotions) to develop more intimate communication with God. There is also a list of resources in the Appendix which will direct you to further reading material on the subjects covered.

Summary:

1. The problems we experience in life are opportunities to know God experientially.

2. Right worship is recognizing and valuing God for Who He really is: the most important and worthy Person in our lives.

3. We were created to know and worship God, and this is what changes us to be more like Him.

4. We need to address our problems in light of how we view and relate to God.

5. Intimacy with God leads to satisfaction and joy in life.

Copyright 1998, 2001, 2005, 2007, 2019, 2020 Scope Ministries International, INC.

A Life Transformed, con't.

In the midst of that crisis, God opened my heart to see Him as He really is and myself as He sees me. I had doubted the everyday involvement of God in my life, but I began to recognize that some things aren't just a coincidence but are the evidence of His involvement with me personally. I finally realized that I can know that God loves me because He made the ultimate sacrifice of His Son, not because my life is free from problems. I experienced His love and care and peace in the darkest days of my life. I know that He is the only reason that I survived the last few years of separation and then the rebuilding of our marriage. In this whole process, He has changed me.

As a performer, I was always very concerned with pleasing people. I'm not nearly as compulsive as I used to be. When I had to choose between my parent's wishes or plans and my husband's plans, my parents always won because I was so worried about what they would think of me. Last Christmas I took a huge step. I chose not to visit my parents because I knew it wasn't best for my family. That spoke volumes to Jeff to show that I was valuing him over my extended family. If this had happened before, I would have felt very guilty for disappointing them. Now I can make decisions that are best for my marriage and family because I do not find my identity in the approval of everyone else.

On Mother's Day, my kids each gave me a card that listed things they thought about me like my favorite song, my favorite movie, etc. One sentence read "my mother loves me best when...," and my son Jordan wrote "my mother loves me best all the time." This reinforced to me that God feels that way about me. He can't get disappointed with me. My actions and choices may affect the quality of my life, but His love for me is not going to change. That's how I feel about God. No matter what I do, He loves me best all the time.

Shari - Nurse

A Transformed Life - Day One

Goal: To recognize how my response to my problems reveals my view of God.

1. Read over the funnel chart explanation on pages 218-219 in this lesson.

2. Funnel a present situation that you are struggling with using the blank funnel provided.

USING THE "FUNNEL CHART"

Ask the Holy Spirit to guide your thoughts. Complete the left side of the funnel chart in regard to the feelings and actions in your life. Begin by thinking of a situation that really bothered you this past week or month.

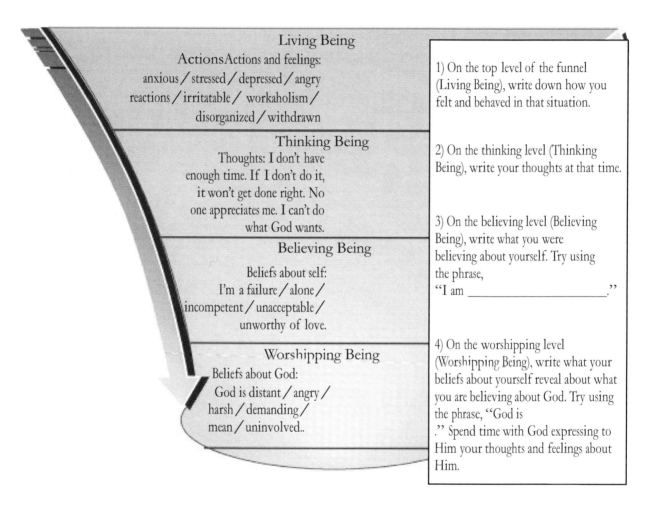

5) Now, go back up the right side of the funnel chart. At the worshipping level, contrast your negative beliefs about God to what is true about Him. Give Scripture references. Stop and reject the lies you have been believing about God, and thank Him for Who He really is. (You may not feel this yet, but it is true nevertheless.) Refer Day 2 of The Truth about the Heavenly Father for truths about God relating to us.

6) On the believing level, write what is true about you in light of God's Word and His character. (Look at the Lesson The Truth about Your New Identity). Acknowledge to God the lies you have been believing about yourself, and replace the lies with the truth.

7) On the thinking level, write what thoughts will result from your new beliefs about God and yourself.

8) On the living level, write what behaviors will result from your new beliefs about God and yourself. Your feelings will eventually follow. Ask the Holy Spirit what step of faith (an action, belief to accept, attitude to be willing to change, etc.) He wants you to take.

A Transformed Life - Day Two

Goal: To recognize how God wants to make Himself personally known to you in the midst of life's problems.

1. Look back to "Summary" at the end of each lesson. List the ones about which God has given you a greater understanding.

2. What changes are resulting from your new understanding of these truths?

3. Read over "Problem Solving in Light of Who God Is" on the next page and then list the characteristics of God that He wants to reveal to you through your present problems.

4. Spend time worshipping God for Who He is.

PROBLEM SOLVING IN LIGHT OF WHO GOD IS

GOD IS COMPASSIONATE - He cares about all of my problems, and He cares about me. He feels my pain. (2 Corinthians 1:3; 1 Peter 5:7).

GOD IS OMNIPOTENT - He is able to solve my problems. Nothing is too hard for Him, and no problem is too big. Through Him I can do all things (Philippians 4:13).

GOD IS OMNISCIENT - He knows all about my problems, and He knows the solution. He has already planned to work these problems together for my good (Romans 8:28-29).

GOD IS WISE - He allowed this problem in my life because He knows what is best for me, and He also knows the best solution.

GOD IS OMNIPRESENT - As I face problems, He is with me and in me. He never asks me to solve problems by myself. The living God is my Helper (Isaiah 41:10; Matthew 28:20; Hebrews 13:5,6).

GOD IS IMMUTABLE (NEVER CHANGING) - The same God Who saved me (solved my biggest problem) is able to help me in whatever problem I face. The God Who helped David, Daniel, Paul, etc., in their problems is the same God Who is able to help me. I can always count on God being God (Hebrews 13:8).

GOD IS SOVEREIGN - He is in complete control of the situation. He allowed this problem to come into my life. Both my problem and I are in His loving hands.

GOD IS FAITHFUL - As I trust God for the solution to this problem, He will not fail me. His promises cannot fail. I can rely on God in this situation. God is absolutely trustworthy, dependable, and reliable. (2 Corinthians 1:20)

GOD IS TRUE - I can trust God's promises in His Word because God does not and cannot lie! What He says He will do, He will do! (Numbers 23:19; Titus 1:2)

GOD IS ETERNAL - As I view my problems in light of eternity, they become quite insignificant (Deuteronomy 33:27; 2 Corinthians 4:17).

GOD IS GOOD - In the midst of my problems and difficulties, God wants to bless me. He wants to make me more like Jesus (Romans 8:28-29).

GOD IS RIGHTEOUS - In allowing these problems to come into my life, God did what was right. God makes no mistakes!

GOD IS LOVE - God wants to reveal His love to me through these problems. There is no problem, no matter how great, that can separate me from His love (Romans 8:35-39).

GOD IS JUST - God is absolutely just in all that He does, including allowing these problems in my life.

GOD IS IN THE MIDST OF PRESSURES AND PROBLEMS! (Exodus 33:14; Deuteronomy 4:29-31; 31:8; Isaiah 43:10-11).

A Transformed Life - Day Three

Goal: To identify areas where you need to grow in understanding and faith.

1. Read over the "Summary" at the end of each lesson. List the key points which you do not fully understand.

2. Spend some time asking God to help you understand them.

A Transformed Life - Day Four

Goal: To review what God has taught you through these lessons.

1. What did God identify as one of the major root problem(s) in your life?

2. What faulty beliefs did God reveal to you?

3. How has your perspective of yourself changed?

4. How has your perspective of God changed?

5. How has your perspective of living the Christian life changed?

6. What are some lies the enemy uses against you to rob you of joy and peace?

7. What truth have you learned to combat these schemes?

8. What is your part in building an intimate relationship with God?

9. Spend a few minutes thanking God for all that He has taught you and for the changes you see Him making in your life.

A Transformed Life - Day Five

Goal: To make a plan for continuing to renew your mind with God's truth.

1. Read through "Additional Helps for the Renewing Process" on the page 234. Check the ones that stand out to you as possible future assignments.

2. Of those you checked, with which will you start? Schedule a time to get started.

3. Which of the assignments you checked needs to be an ongoing lifestyle change? Ask the Holy Spirit to motivate, empower, and remind you to implement these changes.

A Life Transformed - Lesson Nine - Summary

Name - _____
Date - _____

Answer the following questions. To turn in page to small group leader..

1. What has been the most significant thing God has revealed to you through this nine-week study?

2. How has this truth begun to change your life?

3. How has God worked in your life during your Discovery Group experience?

4. What is one area of your life in which you would like to experience transformation?

5. Mark the graph to indicate how much of this week's assignment you completed.

None ———————————————50%————————————————100%

Copyright 1998, 2001, 2005, 2007, 2019, 2020 Scope Ministries International, INC.

Additional Helps for the Renewing Process

What you have learned and applied in these nine lessons is only the beginning of the renewal process. The following are some suggestions to help you continue on in this process.

1. Read the Bible with the single purpose of seeing Who God is. It is helpful to start with a Bible that has not been written in, and with a color highlighter, highlight each verse that reveals something about the character of God. Start in the Gospels and then go to the Psalms (John is an excellent place to start).

2. Keep a personal notebook to record the lies that God reveals to you that need to be put off and the truth that needs to be put on. This will be a good reference tool when encountering future problems.

3. Practice meditating on the Truth and "Truth talk." Meditating simply means "to think about something." Truth-talking is the practice of telling yourself the Truth and praying the Truth back to God. Psalm 23 is a good example of this type of prayer. Start by praying back Scripture, personalizing it in your own words.

4. Develop the habit of meditating on the Truth by writing down a specific helpful Truth on a 3 x 5 card and carrying this with you. Connect meditating on this Truth with another repetitive practice, such as getting a drink, eating a meal, or going to the bathroom. Soon you will have the Truth cemented into your thinking.

5. On 3x5 index cards the characteristics of God for which your faith is the weakest. As needs or fears arise, practice Truth-talking about God as your Father.

6. Continue to practice putting off the lies you have believed about yourself as revealed in The Truth about Your New Identity. Use one of the methods mentioned in #4 and #5.

7. Practice keeping a REED journal (Freedom with Emotions). Be sure to record the date and circumstances that prompted the negative feelings. This will help you recognize if there is a pattern to these negative emotions. Be sure to work all the way through REED to the "evaluate" and "decide" steps; otherwise, all you will accomplish is obtaining a little relief from suppressing your emotions. Record the lies you have believed and the truth from God's perspective.

8. Make worship a lifestyle. Pray Scripture back to God. Sing songs of praise and worship to God. Practice "doing" the Psalms instead of just reading them. Listen to and sing along with praise and worship music. This will help you focus on God instead of yourself and your circumstances. Talk to God about everything, as you would your closest friend.

9. Read Christian books and listen to teaching tapes that will reinforce the truth that you have learned through this workbook. Look over the Suggested Reading list and check the books that would help reinforce the truths you need to focus on. You cannot hear the truth too much. Remember how long you have listened to the lies.

10. Fellowship with other believers who are seeking to know God and grow in their new identity. It is imperative that you stay connected and involved with people in the Body of Christ who will pray for you and encourage you in your faith. Standing alone against your three-fold enemy is very difficult.

11. Remember, your goal is to know God experientially in the midst of life's problems and to allow God to transform you into Christ-likeness. To "seek first the kingdom of God and His righteousness" begins by receiving God's unconditional love for you. Make it a habit to spend a few minutes several times each day receiving God's love. This is not a time of Bible study or prayer but a time to be still and know that He is God and to receive His love by faith.

12. Share with others what God is teaching you and what He is doing in your life. Giving to others what God has freely given you will reinforce the truth in your own life.

13. Daily practice consciously and verbally yielding your expectations and rights to God. Trust Him to meet your needs in the very best way and at the right time.

14. Practice asking yourself and God two questions: What are You doing in my life? What do You want me to do? Expect God to speak to you through His Word and through His indwelling Spirit. We do not have to live in continual confusion or bondage. When you have trouble discerning the answer to these two questions, talk to someone whom you respect for his walk with God. None of us hears God perfectly all the time. That's why we need to stay connected to the Body.

15. Reread the lessons in this workbook, and work through the specific assignments that address your particular needs.

Remember that this is an ongoing, moment-by-moment, lifelong process.

Suggested Reading

Belief Systems/Renewing the Mind:

"A Study of the Mind," booklet - Preston and Anabel Gillham

Search for Freedom - Robert McGee Search for Significance - Robert McGee

Sidetracked in the Wilderness - Michael Wells

The Good News/God's Forgiveness

The Gift of Forgiveness - Charles Stanley

"Forgiven Forever," booklet - Bob George

"Grace to Forgive" Scott Hadden

"Forgiveness" Steve Eden

Seeing Yourself as God Sees You:

"Unleashing Your Passion for God" Scott Hadden

Lifetime Guarantee - Bill Gillham

Classic Christianity - Bob George

"He Loves Me" Wayne Jacobsen-

Living Free in Christ - Neil Anderson

What is the Father Like? - W. Phillip Keller

Your Parents and You - McGee, Springle & Craddock

Let God Love You - Malcolm Smith

The Healing Heart of God - Malcolm Smith

The Father Heart of God - Floyd McClung

Emotions/Guilt, Anger, Forgiveness:

Healing for Damaged Emotions - David Seamands

Where is God When it Hurts? - Philip Yancey

Freedom of Forgiveness - David Augsburger

"Anger, Fear in Disguise," booklet - Bob George

Forgiveness - Malcolm Smith

Search for Peace - Robert McGee

Growing in Grace - Bob George

Grace Walk - Steve McVey

The Promise - Tony Evans

The Secret to the Christian Life - Gene Edwards

Tired of Trying to Measure Up - Jeff VanVonderen

Grace Works - Dudley Hall

This workbook and the above resources are available through the Scope Resource Center:
700 NE 63rd Street, Oklahoma City, OK 73105-6410
405.843.7778. www.scopeministries.org

(These books and Scope's Teens Transformed workbook, are made available as a service by Scope Ministries International. These are resources to be used in conjunction with the Biblical personal guidance ministry or in the Biblical training program. The inclusion of these books does not imply that Scope is in agreement with all of the contents of these books).

Nature of Man
Appendix
Terms in Brief

These terms are defined as Scope understands and uses them:

1. Old Nature (old Man)

    The old race of fallen man that has been damned because of sins through Adam. The identity with which every descendant of Adam is born. (Romans 5)

2. New Nature (new man)

    The regenerated spirit of the believer. The human spirit made alive by, indwelt by, and united with the Holy Spirit. The new man is Christ's life within regenerate man.

3. Flesh (self-life)

    A condition and tendency within man to operate in his own strength and / or for reasons centered in himself. In the non-Christian it is the natural method of functioning that is, by means of body and soul only. In the Christian it is the selfish inclination to function as though he were body and soul only.

    The flesh may be described as "My claim to my right to myself."

4. Sin

    The deception that fulfillment (needs being met), meaning, and purpose in life may be experienced apart from God. In the Christian it is that unholy principle which indwells him, but is separate from the new man because the new man is the very life of Christ within the believer and sin cannot be part of Christ Himself. All sin was covered and cleansed through the Blood of Christ.

5. Sins

    Acts contrary to the will of God. Actions in man which "fall short" of revealing God's glory. "Sins" are what result when "sin" is obeyed.

Scope Ministries International
www.scopeministries.org

Made in the USA
Columbia, SC
04 January 2025